MOMENTS

MOMENTS

Leadership when it matters most

Zoë Routh

Zoë Routh
zoerouth.com

First published by Inner Compass Australia in December 2016
First Amazon edition February 2017

Zoë Routh asserts the moral right to be identified as the author of *Moments: Leadership when it matters most* and all associated products.

ISBN 978-0-9944119-3-8

Subjects: Success, Fulfilment, Leadership, Mindset, Motivation, Productivity

Author photograph by Oli Sansom – olisansom.com
Edited by Rebecca Stewart – thegallopingskirt.com
Typesetting, book design and printing by bookbound.com.au

For more information about the author
Zoë Routh
Email: zoe@innercompass.com.au
www.**zoerouth**.com

Disclaimer
This book is intended to give general information only. The material herein does not represent professional advice. The author expressly disclaims all liability to any person arising directly or indirectly from the use of, or for any errors or omissions, the information in this book. The adoption and application of the information in this book is at the reader's discretion and is his or her sole responsibility.

Contents

To Rob,

for showing me how to enjoy the moment.

FOREWORD

This is what frustrates me.

When I see good people, smart people, shy away from speaking their mind.

When I see a leader not stepping into the life they truly want out of obligation.

When professionals shoot off an email to vent their spleen.

When leaders cut others down to size.

When executives use email to 'express concerns' or lecture others.

When leaders tell me about how they feel 'stuck' in their life out of duty.

When people gossip and shoot down their peers out of petty jealousy (and when I catch myself doing that too).

Here's the thing.

Your life is made up of moments.

The quality of your life depends on the quality of these moments. And the quality of these moments is completely dependent on how you show up, how you connect, and how you act in each precious moment.

If you are like many leaders I work with, at first it's likely you don't take that kind of care in the moment. It's likely you don't show up with that kind of focus. Yet.

If so, you are burning relationships. You are frittering away your life in petty worries. You're getting passed over because you don't step up and stand out. Because you don't speak your mind. Because you play small instead of living large. Because you are afraid to rock the boat.

Because you are afraid of being seen. Really seen.

And who misses out?

You do. Your family does. Your colleagues do. Your business does.

Every time you shrink instead of expand, you rob the people you care about. Your silence steals ideas and opportunity from your work and hides them away. The world needs each voice and each brilliant light to shine. Every time you hide, you hold the evolution of human consciousness back.

Moments is your handbook to help you speak more clearly, to be seen more strongly, and to be courageous when fear rattles the cage of your heart. I want you to be fierce in your heart, gentle in your presence, and sound in your conviction.

I invite you to lead your life, not just live it.

We can do that – one moment at a time.

Zoë Routh, Canberra 2016

INTRODUCTION

The model of *Moments*

Leadership, real leadership that changes the course of history, happens in a moment. It's the choices we make in these moments that tip the scales. Questions such as: "Do I say what I really think or don't I?"; "Do I speak up or don't I?"; "Do I connect with this stranger or walk on by?"; and "Do I say yes to this opportunity or let it go?" can change everything.

I wrote *Moments* because I watched so many of my clients shrink from who they want to be. I believe this is because they are afraid: afraid to act, afraid to speak up, afraid to be seen. I've watched them struggle as they led lives unfulfilled until they held their toes to the fire. In these moments they find they cannot stand the pain of being less than who they really are, and choose to take a leap of courage.

I also wanted answers for myself! I too found myself shutting down, sometimes biting my tongue, not bothering to speak my opinion, afraid to be seen, afraid of being rejected or criticised. And I felt the slow crippling of a life less than fully lived.

I want more for myself and more for my clients. All of us deserve to live fully in the sunlight, unashamed to be who we are, and fulfilled in the choices we make.

The Seen – Heard – Valued Model

This model describes how we find our voice and take action.

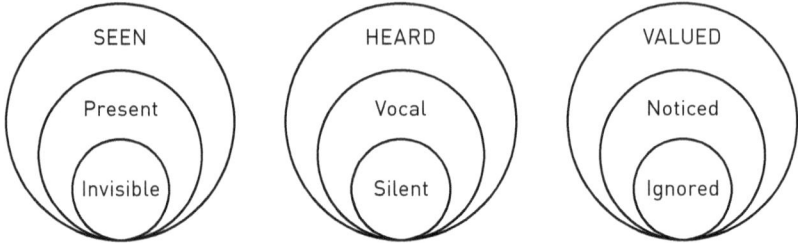

Figure 1: The Seen – Heard – Valued Model

At the bottom end of the spectrum (the smallest circles), we are not centered and we feel vulnerable. Feeling invisible, silent, and ignored, we build no bridges and we are shut down. The professional risk to us is significant. We have no impact or influence, and the frustration turns back on ourselves and eats away at us.

When we find the courage to voice an opinion (as the circles get larger), the risk of being overlooked is cut in half. However, if we do not manage our connection and our messaging properly, we can polarise people. When we do show up, are fully present, and express our opinion, we start to get noticed.

When we manage our emotions, our message, and our intention (the largest circles), we can step in to any difficult moment with confidence. We invite conversation and create connection. These difficult moments become magic moments. We are seen, heard, and valued.

The Influence Model, or how to handle the moments that matter

Being able to exercise this kind of connected leadership in difficult moments takes practice. Like a martial artist, hours in training prepare us for a moment of challenge. We need to hone our Presence, Perspective, and Power.

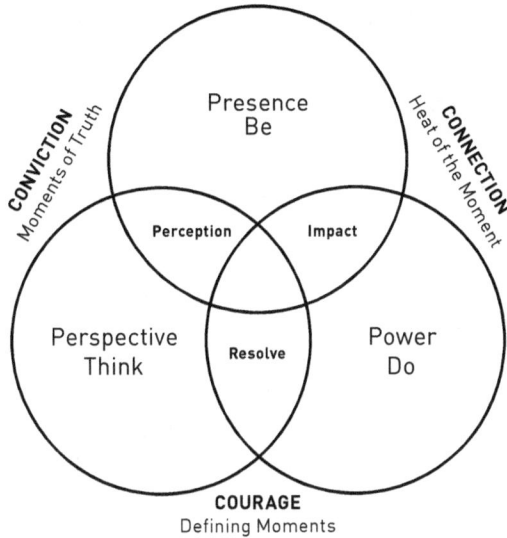

CONVICTION
Moments of Truth

CONNECTION
Heat of the Moment

Presence
Be

Perception

Impact

Perspective
Think

Resolve

Power
Do

COURAGE
Defining Moments

Presence is deep self-mastery of our physical, emotional, mental and spiritual self. It requires quiet contemplation and conscious choices of self-nurture.

Perspective is the length and breadth of our thinking. It's the capacity to consider generations of past influences and the impact of our choices on generations to come. Perspective is about who we hold as stakeholders and the complex systems that weave us together. It's about being world-centric, no matter where we find our feet planted.

Power is about the effort to act. Every time we make a choice based on our values, for the greater good, we strengthen our courage muscle. Leadership becomes less about us, our career aspirations, our paltry personal concerns, and more about how we can help.

Deep presence and an expanded perspective give us powerful **perception**, and conviction to find the best way forward in moments of truth. A broad perspective and a strong sense of power charge our **resolve** and give us courage in defining moments. The edgy power of true grit combined with an anchored presence allow us to show up with positive **impact**, creating strong connections in the heat of the moment.

In the Influence Model, our influence evolves from developing these three leadership superpowers:

- **Perception:** The ability to see deeply in to an issue with far-reaching consequences
- **Resolve:** The courage and tenacity to take action and do something
- **Impact:** Influence and resonance with those we would inspire and encourage.

This is what gives us conviction in our message, the courage to speak, and connection so it lands. Every act of courage lifts us all. Ten thousand acts of courage will actually shift the consciousness of those around us to a happier state of being. And happy humans make a happier world.

When I ask people in my workshops about the moments that matter, they all come back with the following:

- Standing up your boss
- Asking for a promotion
- Speaking up about a matter you believe in
- Asking your partner to marry you
- Saying yes to the proposal
- Telling your partner you want a divorce
- Being there for your kids when they get sick or injured
- Being there for your kids when they have a concert, presentation, or a parent-teacher meeting
- Smelling the roses
- Playing with the chickens (that one's mine!)

These are the moments that matter. Through Perception, Resolve, and Impact, these moments are expressed in three ways.

Perception

In *Moments* we will look at where our perception is most needed, when we need to make a choice about our personal challenges, and what these mean for us at our core.

These are called **Moments of Truth**:

- Bridging moments
- Crucible moments
- Rock bottom moments.

Moments of Truth (personal)

Personal moments are when we are confronted with who we are, our failings, our challenges, and our shadow. We need to decide if we will live up to the best version of ourselves, or not. These are Moments of Truth.

They often appear as Crucible Moments and Rock Bottom Moments as well. It's when things get really terrible and somehow we have to scrape our way through to feel better, learn from it, and make amends. Joseph Campbell in his book *The Hero With a Thousand Faces* [1] (1949) describes these experiences as essential to the Hero's Journey. The Hero ventures forth into the unknown and comes face to face with their self, often depicted as a monster. In stories such as Jonah and the Whale, Jonah is swallowed by the whale and must fight and find his way out. This has become the euphemism for when we are at the darkest stage of our own self-doubts and despair. This is the real guts of the Hero's Journey, where we are in the belly of the whale and must fight our way out, lest we get digested by the pain from the inside out.

The voice we need at this Moment of Truth is our own inner voice. How we talk to each other and guide ourselves through it is the critical make up of our resolve and perspective in these pivotal moments.

Resolve

We will explore the moments that require expanded perspective and deep courage. This is when we need fine-tuned resolve.

These are called **Defining Moments**:

- · Challenges to our leadership
- · Challenges to our values
- · Between a rock and a hard place
- · Speaking up.

Defining Moments (ethical)

Ethical moments are where our values are challenged and all choices feel bad. These are otherwise known as a 'rock and a hard place'. Neither choice feels like a win, and part of us feels we will lose something. Usually we end up metaphorically sawing a hand off like Aaron Ralston, the survivor of a canyoneering accident.[2] Some part of our ruined 'hand' (or sense of self) is left behind in these moments, and we need to find a way to heal and move on, blemished and scarred. The good news is that if we do deep preparation and deep self-understanding work, we are better able to make these defining decisions without losing too much of our integrity, reputation, or tribe.

Impact

Finally we will examine moments where need our impact most, where we need to have the best connection. These are called the **Heat of the Moment.**

Heat of the Moment (interpersonal)

Interpersonal moments are when we get caught up with other people. This is the messiness of relationships: personal, professional, and the awkward ones with strangers. These moments press all our buttons. When we engage with others we feel ferociously, we interpret (and misinterpret) messages and actions, and we work to have ourselves seen, heard, and valued. These are often the toughest moments because there are things we can control: (ourselves) and things we cannot (others). These kinds of moments are when we need to manage ourselves the most, and where we can often blow up or shut down. These are high stakes situations and where we need great personal power and a broad perspective to handle the torrent of emotions.

– ☐ –

This is a book that encourages greater humanity. It defines leadership as a practice, the practice of connection between human beings. And connection only happens in moments, not meetings. Either we connect in moments or we don't, and the moment is lost forever.

Moments encompasses the polarity of these points in time; the deep dive within that allows wide expansion and connections to be made. It focuses on what it takes to make the right choices in the moments that matter most. It's part personal triumph (what to do in 'do or die' moments), part mindfulness, how to have grace under fire, and part leadership handbook.

This book is not about shining bright and advancing one's own career agenda. It is about being the kind of leader who cuts through with connection and diverts disaster through their very presence and the choices they make on the spot.

The key premise is how to build oneself as a leadership lightning rod in the storm of chaos. *Moments* describes all the preparation and habits required to build leadership capacity across personal and global contexts, and to be able to handle the extremes of turbulence, in the moment. It's the balance of leadership being (mindfulness), leadership thinking (strategy), and leadership doing (execution).

As you move through these pages, you will find the courage to walk your talk, say what you mean, and do the right thing.

So, strap on your boots. Let's seize the moment.

PART ONE

Context

1. Leadership context

Leadership is a deeply personal expression. Formed by cultural pressures and immediate contextual forces, we also must consider the historical and global trends that drive an even bigger picture of leadership. When we become aware of all these forces, we begin to manage how we lead.

Voice, our ability to express what we really feel and think, is the lifeblood of leading a fulfilling life. If we are not fully self-expressed, we are like a plant growing in shadows, reaching for the light; a little bent and crippled.

When we find our voice we learn how to speak up, to speak out, and speak with others. We get seen, heard, and valued. No matter how terrifying or dangerous we may find them, we feel stronger as we give voice to our innermost thoughts. Hiding our thoughts is hiding a part of ourselves, and ultimately we know we are living a lie.

Being able to speak our truth is liberating. To own the fullness of who we are is like being able to dance naked in full sunlight with absolutely no fear. It's not quite the feeling of reckless abandon, but of considered freedom.

The people around us are so thirsty for us to speak the truth. When we hear someone speak up for themselves and own their perspective in a gracious manner, we are in turn illuminated, and given permission or invited to be honest, to be genuine, to be authentic. We crave it. Over years of socialisation we have learned to hide away our inner thoughts because they offend, or they frighten, or they don't fit the status quo. We've invented a whole range of reasons for staying quiet and shutting down.

So what gets in our way of speaking up?

I have a Google alert for 'speaking up'. At least twice a day I read pieces from people who write of the obstacles, consequences, and the outcomes of speaking up. This is usually against an injustice. From afar, we give a nod to those who put themselves in the crossfire for a higher cause. We deem them noble and brave. And we like to think we would do the same.

But would we?

Here are four 'types' of people who don't speak up:

The Pleaser

The Pleaser's excuses are masked by their good intentions. They want to make a positive contribution, and hesitate unless they are sure their voice will be welcome. Their real issue is lack of confidence.

The Wounded

The Wounded's catch cry is: "They're an asshole." It is the 'get out of jail free' excuse for not confronting a nemesis. The Wounded dismisses the object of their derision as unworthy of any effort, because they are simply less of a person than we are, due to their aberrant behaviour. The Wounded's reluctance to deal with 'assholes' robs them of the opportunity to develop capacity for compassion and empathy. With a narrow view, The Wounded disables their ability to be influential and make good decisions.

The Rationalist

The Rationalist is crippled by: "There's too much at stake." They feel there are genuine risks in speaking up and out. The Rationalist feels they may ruffle feathers or tilt the scales. There may be outright rebuffs, dressing down, alienation, ostracism, even sabotage. They feel they may lose their job, reputation, or relationships. The problem here is that the Rationalist may fail to act on their moral compass. They put self-preservation above doing the right thing.

The Apathetic

"The Apathetic's cry "I'm too tired to care" is insidious. They are so worn out by the pace of their actual and digital lives they do not have the capacity to follow through important leadership commitments. The Apathetic's willpower battery is drained dry from decision fatigue; from the millions of tiny decisions we need to make. What surprise then that the Apathetic's lifestyle and work style leave little room for the bigger leadership choices? Speak up? Who can be bothered.

By not speaking up, The Pleaser, The Wounded, The Rationalist and The Apathetic in all of us lose our integrity. These are high stakes games. Learning to speak up, out and with others takes particular skill, and is something we will unpack in *Moments*.

2. The risks when we get leadership wrong

Reputation

We are known by *how* we show up as much what we say and do. How we deliver the message and the energy of our presence either detracts from or supports the message. And our reputation alongside it.

Kevin Rudd, the former Australian Prime Minister, had no problem speaking his mind. Everyone knew what he thought and felt. His opinion was obvious because he tended to broadcast it, like a thunderstorm through a megaphone. He was explosive and derisive. He once yelled at a flight attendant because his special meal was not available. His staff kept their heads down and ran for cover. He was tyrannical in his demands and equally turgid in his reprimands. He 'spoke his truth', but the truth is he became known for having the temper of a tyrant. His reputation earned him no friends and little respect.

What was Kevin Rudd's leadership legacy? He is remembered as someone who did not master himself and had little care and compassion for others. His reputation erased any of his political convictions and achievements, even if they were motivated from a noble purpose. Rudd's legacy is one of a besmirched reputation. By blowing up, he shut others down.

Relationships

If we always say what we think and feel in relationships, we might get branded with any number of names, from 'traitor', to 'disloyal' to 'shit-stirrer' or 'self-serving'.

I've been called all of these names after attempting to 'speak my truth' about what I saw and felt. At a meeting of executives, I raised what I saw was an important strategic issue for the company: business viability. My intention was to raise this as an important leadership concern that we should all take responsibility for. I had hoped we would rally together to work on the issue and put forward a cohesive problem-solving plan.

When I first announced: "I think there is too little business to support this number of staff" I was met with stony silence. Then panic, anger, and sabotage ensued.

Speaking your truth does not just mean dumping bad news on the table. This tends to act as a 'poo bomb' – it lands and splatters over everyone, including the speaker. Relationships suffer. When done well, speaking your truth is a more considered affair, where we think deeply about our own perspective as well as others.

Impact

When not checking our intentions, we can really misfire. The things that dribble out of our mouths have unintended consequences, simply because we did not take a moment to focus our intention for a positive impact.

James [3] is an accomplished, forward-thinking CEO. His views are progressive, and push the bounds of innovation. Not everyone on the board moves as quickly as James. They are often in conflict with him over the pace and nature of changes he wishes to introduce. James finds this frustrating, and experiences the opposition on the board as holding him back and being unwilling to move with the times.

After a while, James managed to get one of his key initiatives off the ground, with some initial successful outcomes. At the next board meeting, these successes were grudgingly acknowledged by the various board members. After the meeting, James sidled up to his most vocal opponent and calmly mentioned that it was a good thing they had gone with James's idea after all. A bit of "I told you so".

While he was not overtly aggressive as per his usual style, defaulting to passive aggressiveness was not much of an improvement. James was not building rapport or trust with his board members, but playing alpha games – a business version of 'might is right'.

The intention to slap someone down divides rather than unites people. Though we may win small victories by feeling vindicated, we actually lose the long-term game as we erode our capacity for influence through respect. Intentions need to be checked for genuineness.

3. What broader influences stop us from leading in moments that matter?

Lack of Presence

We invest our attention on the future at the expense of the present. Our 'future focus' looks to far horizons, but ensures we can't see and feel where we're standing right now.

We are leading with great forward-thinking strategy and detailed planning. We spend countless hours in meetings pondering our future options; projecting our future results. The surge is always to the anticipated rewards of the future.

But where we are failing to lead is right now. Right now, in this rare and precious moment.

Our future focus drives us to wallow in these self-perceived limitations: Are we good enough to live up to expectations? Are we capable of delivering on such huge plans? What if they find us lacking? What if they figure out we have no idea what we're really doing? Doubt causes hesitation.

Our future focus sets us adrift in loneliness. All our happiness is staked on some future state. We agonise about it in our own private chamber of pain. We can't admit this to anyone, of course, because that would give the impression we weren't up to it. We think that the future – our future – will get passed to someone else.

Our future focus is rife with fantasy and worry. We worry about the future; we worry about the past. We worry about what Bob thought of our presentation. We worry about how Jane will perceive our work project. We worry where the next client will come from, if the neighbours will like our dinner party, if the dog will get over her midnight barking.

Our future focus makes us hungry for happiness. We reach ever forward and find that happiness slippery like an eel. We strive and push and struggle to get our goals. When and if we get there, we pant exhausted, only to stumble towards the next target, groaning. The future is ever in the future.

Lack of Purpose

Our future focus is also a symptom of 'achievement disease'. This is destructive if not kept in check.

The compulsion to achieve is stamped firmly in our cultural consciousness. From the moment we wriggle in to the world, we are measured against milestones. We wonder if the baby is crawling, talking, and eating within the top percentile. In school we are graded for our performance. We are benchmarked against national standards. Even our clothes have different categories to rate us and drive our sense of self-worth.

At work we slot into a hierarchy, and each year we need to meet performance targets in order to progress and receive rewards. No progress? No rewards. No performance? No recognition.

Our achievement disease is also bound up in our biochemistry.

We are hardwired to seek it out. As cave dwellers, we needed to hunt to survive, and that took effort. Our biochemistry helped promote our survival by flooding our system with endorphins after we chased down prey. The endorphins helped us to get up and hunt again, to expend the energy to get the reward; the food and the endorphins.

The survival of our species was helped by feeling good about achieving. The rush of deadlines is the modern version of chasing down our prey.

Dopamine is another achievement by-product. Dopamine gets released every time we find what we're looking for, finish something, or get what we set out to get. It's part of a savvy search, risk, and reward system. Every time we find something or get something we want, we get a little surge of feel-good. This is why emails, texting, task lists, and video games can develop compulsive behaviour.[4] We get hooked on that little hit of achievement. It's a great sense of satisfaction and it is incredibly addictive. Dopamine is the real juice behind our achievement disease.

Our achievement disease is linked to social acceptance: reach these standards and be part of our club. This fires up our oxytocin – the feel-good chemical that is about belonging and the safety of group identity. Oxytocin is that feeling of love we get from our partner, or between mother and child, or in well-bonded teams. It's the warm blanket of social safety and the protection of the tribe.

Achievement is linked to personal acceptance: if you get those grades, Mum and Dad will be proud. Win that tender and the board will give you an award. Serotonin is one of the other feel-good biochemicals at work here. Serotonin is also known as the 'happiness chemical'. We get it from approval, pride, and recognition.

From a biochemical point of view, achievement is the full package: it delivers on addictive endorphins and dopamine, and it sweetens the pot with oxytocin and serotonin.

Why is it causing so much trouble?

The pressure to perform is so deeply seductive that it drives individuals and teams to cheat. The desire to achieve becomes 'results at all costs'. Achievement becomes about the ends justifying the means. This drive to achieve, this achievement disease, was what derailed ethics at Enron, an energy company in Houston, Texas.

As CEO, Jeffrey Skilling formed a staff of executives who exploited loopholes, fudged financial reporting, and hid debt from failed deals. He lied to and deceived his board, all under the banner of achievement, producing results, and performing. It became the largest bankruptcy re-organisation in American history at that time.[5] He was convicted of several US federal felonies and was sentenced to 24 years in prison and fined US $45 million.[6]

Probably the starkest example of ethical derailment is the story of Jordan Belfort, whose autobiography was depicted in Martin Scorsese's film *The Wolf of Wall Street* (2013). The drive to achieve and win became a compulsion that overrode many moral boundaries. Drug addiction, corruption, deception, degradation. It was all about winning the business game.

In Germany, the CEO of Volkswagen Martin Winterkorn resigned. He "took responsibility" for the decision to install software in its diesel cars in the US, software that was designed to evade emissions tests. Though he continues to assert there was no personal wrongdoing in the incident,[7] Volkswagen announced that as a result of the emissions scandal,[8] it will recall 8.5 million cars in Europe (including 2.4 million in Germany), 1.2 million in the UK and 500,000 in the US.

Whether the CEO knew explicitly of the software deception or not, leadership failed at Volkswagen. A culture that allows its people to deceive authorities, its customers, and the public has some serious faults in the moral compass. Somewhere in Volkswagon, a group of people decided that deception for results was more important than integrity. This is a leadership failure that can be traced back to its leader and to his leadership. He failed to create a culture that lives its values of 'responsibility' and 'sustainability' and avoiding the great pressures to achieve.

Achievement disease can cost us our life. Athletes, executives, and video gamers make the news broadcasts for dropping dead and stumbling towards the finish line. Even the marathon, a benchmark of human effort, commemorates the run of the Greek soldier Pheidippides, a messenger from the Battle of Marathon to Athens. After running without water or pause he delivers the good news of victory, and promptly dies.

Achievement disease blinkers us to what matters most, including our own life.

Lack of Perspective

If achievement disease draws our focus forward, ego drives our perspective inwards. We ponder our personal concerns until this becomes the lens through which we see the world: the 'navel lens.'

Seeing the world through the navel lens stunts our perspective and pinches our ability for influence. We are so concerned about saving our own backsides that we loosen the grip on our purpose.

From 2010-2015, Australia had five Prime Ministers. Three of the changes were the governing party's mid-term swap of leader. This churn is even greater than Greece, which had only four changes of leaders in the same time period (granted, three of these changes were in the same year, and Greece was facing down national bankruptcy).

What is Australia's excuse? It survived the Global Financial Crisis relatively unscathed. There was no violent political turmoil. Australia ranks second in the world behind Norway for quality of life.[9]

So why the ruthless toppling of leaders?

They failed in their perspective. While politics should be driven by policy, personality and polls now trump purpose. Our politicians have lost sight of the real game: to serve the nation, not themselves. They are a collection of egos vying for the captain's chair. They failed to build a team and inspire a common agenda. Their perception that popularity and approval were the primary objectives (the ends justifying the means) diverted their focus from delivering real results.

Perspective scuppered perception.

Globally, we are seeing narrow perspectives shake cities with violence. Conflict flares with black and white perceptions: "We're right and you're wrong". This 'duality perspective' reduces human civilisation to a fight to death over resources, identity, and ideology.

Duality perspectives set up win-lose scenarios. They are driven by the instinct to survive, which is based on the innate premise that the dominant group survives. It is also based on the primal fear of the unknown, of the 'other' we do not know. The uncertainty of not recognising the other, not understanding their ways, their language, their clothes and even their appearance, creates suspicion and fear. This is one of the reasons why the flood of refugees fleeing Syria has caused so much fear: the unknown frightens us.

The navel lens is short-sighted and dangerous.

There is, however, an alternative perspective. The interconnected world shows that when we collaborate, we all win. In *From Me to We*,[10] Janine Garner writes: "Business leaders and entrepreneurs have the complex responsibility of constant strategic thinking. If those finely-tuned minds can be brought together for mutual benefit, the possibilities expand and the rewards can be dramatically amplified." That two minds are better than one is a simple premise. Two and more different kinds of minds with a world-centric purpose is the innovation platform that not only business, but also the world needs.

As a species, we are intricately connected by our economies, our technology, and our common need to manage the resources of our one planet. Notwithstanding the aspiration to colonise Mars by Elon Musk and others,[11] Earth is all we have, and we're in this together.

We need leaders who can lead from a world-centric perspective. We need leaders who see all communities as part of the global community. We need leaders who see our commonalities and can bridge our differences as a result. We need leaders with one eye fixed on the future we are co-creating and the other on the world in which we are co-existing.

We need the leader in the moment, not the leader of the moment. We need leaders who can be present, connect their team, and connect with others from a place of purpose and contribution.

Lack of Power

I see leaders in their most important moments shy away from being the leader that their teams need. These leaders are sheltering from the storm.

We walk past poor behaviour. We keep quiet when we should speak up. We keep our head down when we should put our hand up. We shrink from making decisions. We agonise over pros and cons when decisions are needed. We let a colleague struggle along without checking in or lending a hand.

We coast through leadership development programs, then slide the materials on to a shelf to gather dust. We play around in workshops, in case studies, roleplays, and exercises, and let it all slip away.

Why?

It's not that we lack commitment to our roles: we are very dedicated and want to do the best job possible. It's not that we lack intelligence or ability: we are high level, competent people. It's not that we are too busy. Though we have punishing work and personal schedules, we are masters of execution.

We cross our fingers and hope poor behaviour will fix it itself. And in the meantime, team trust and enthusiasm are being grated away. Some of us shy away from conflict because we don't want to ruffle feathers.

Why do we fail to capitalise on training and opportunity?

Disavowal. Some of us are so overwhelmed by our own lives that we fail to expand our sense of responsibility beyond immediate obligations:

> "It's someone else's problem."

> "What can I do about it?

> "It's too big an issue for me."

> "I've got to look after myself here."

Some of us cling to our lens on the world as the one and only truth, and become blind to opportunities. We become blind to hardship. We become blind to the past, future, and present alike. We start to believe our own internal voice of personal and petty concerns. Our focus is inward. And we are tethered by our perspective like a domesticated elephant chained to its post.

Confusion. The volume, speed, and multiplicity of information is a cacophony. Our attention is buffeted by distraction. We have flabby focus and our leadership health is suffering.

One report lists the following data created online every day: [12]

- · 500 million tweets sent each day
- · Over 4 million hours of content uploaded to YouTube every day

- Over 1 billion minutes of Vine videos watched each day
- 4.3 billion Facebook messages posted daily
- 5.75 billion Facebook likes every day
- 40 million tweets shared each day
- 6 billion daily Google searches.

With all these increases in social media, email isn't going away any time soon! According to The Radacati Group, in 2015, 205 billion emails were sent each day, and by 2019 that number will increase 20 per cent to 246 billion emails each day.

Distraction creates confusion. And confusion impedes any kind of leadership thinking, being and doing.

Hesitation. We hesitate, catastrophise and feel overwhelmed by consequences. We are so caught up in our heads that we have forgotten about our hearts. We try to do the pros and cons. We weigh up the 'what ifs' and fret over the 'if onlys'.

Consider your choice of coffee in the morning. If you are an inner-city type, you may have your own espresso maker with your favourite eco-friendly, socially-responsible coffee bean grinds at the ready. Or you may have a Nespresso coffee maker. At the time of writing, there are 19 types of Nespresso capsules to choose from. Should you wish to add milk, there are over 80 brands and types of milk on offer in Australian supermarkets.

We are spoiled for choice, and our choices are spoiling.

Internet lore puts the amount of decisions we make each day at 35,000. It could be anything from what to eat, to what to wear, or which way to drive to work. Let alone the more weighty ones: 'Should I leave my husband?'; 'How do I reprimand Drew for his inappropriate comments in last week's meeting?'; or 'Is it time to put the cat down with her diabetes getting extreme?'

We burn up our decision-making energy on the banal and leave little for what matters, especially in moments that matter. All this leaves us disconnected from our self, from others, and from the world. In our self-imposed isolation cell, we experience a crisis of confidence.

How can we put our current leadership situation into a historic framework? And what do we move through the new landscape?

4. A changed leadership landscape

Fifty years ago, the context for leadership changed. The dynamic interplay of economic, social, environmental systems, and globalisation started to shift. How do we compare today's complex movements with what was happening in the world of leadership 50 years ago?

In 1956, world events were transformative: World War II had been over for a decade, there was a newfound optimism, people were busy pumping out babies, and the Vietnam War was just commencing. Elvis hit the charts for the first time with *Heartbreak Hotel*, Norma Jean legally changed her name to Marilyn Monroe, the hard disk drive was invented by an IBM team, and TV commenced broadcasting in Australia. Steve Jobs was born in 1955. Mark Zuckerberg would not be born for another 30 years.

In 1956, planning was linear: Leaders tackled strategy with a 10-year business plan. Milestones were marked out, from point A to point B. Ready, steady, march.

In 1956, company focus was local: Very few companies were global. The 100 top Fortune 500 companies were largely oil, steel, and air transport companies. It was all about power and travel. Now, in 2016, the top Fortune 500 company is Walmart, Apple is listed at number 15, and Amazon is listed 88. Distribution these days is king in global business: how can I get more things to more people more quickly?

In 1956, engagement was straightforward: Businesses used the telephone and letters to connect. In comparison with today, interpersonal connection was more primary, more useful, often more practical, and possibly more powerful.

Trends affecting our capacity to lead like we did in 1956

Amplified Biology

Trans-humanists are already playing with technology. They are creating devices to embed in their body that allows them to open doors, turn on lights, switch on heaters, and even use their bus pass from a chip implanted under the skin in the web between thumb and forefinger. From Verily Life Sciences' work on glucose-sensing contact lenses to the work exploring the ability to upload thoughts and feelings to the internet, great strides are being made to increase our connection. With these new bio-machine interfaces, we potentially have the ability to viscerally magnify our human connections.

Neil Harbisson is the world's first 'official' cyborg. Neil is totally colour blind and only sees the world in shades of grey. In 2004 he had an antenna implanted at the back of his skull that vibrates in response to different colour shades in his environment, allowing him to 'see' vibrationally. The antenna arches over his head and has a little camera lens at eye level. The antenna can also connect to satellites, which allows him to access the internet and to receive videos and messages. Currently there are only five people on the planet allowed to send him messages. As you can imagine, a deluge of email going 'ping' in your skull is currently beyond our biological ability to process and stay sane.

What does all this mean for leadership with presence and focus? With so much dictation and stimulation potentially embedded in our bodies we need the ability to stay calm and present more than ever. Imagine having a bad day, and then that being sent around the planet to your bio-hardware connected contacts.

Communi-pendence

With 40 per cent of the workforce likely to be independent service providers working remotely from cafes and locations around the globe,[13] how we work with each other will shift dramatically. There is a myth that these independent people work solo on projects. In reality, many will team up and collaborate on various projects. Each will take turns leading a project, or supporting it. Leadership will become a game of swapping hats, depending on who is leading what project, under whose banner, and for which client. Open collaboration will be essential for these kinds of workers. There is no room to hide and play obedient foot soldier. The success of these teams will need strong voices, healthy rapport, and good connection – all maintained remotely.

Digi-driven consciousness

Virtual and augmented reality will allow us to explore our sense of humanity and potential in ways we have only imagined beforehand. Everest VR is a new virtual reality game developed for HTC Vive that allows user to strap on headsets and undertake the trek to the top of Everest. Players can cross the ladders over gaping crevasses, walk on a knife's edge with an eight-kilometre drop, and stand on the world's rooftop. At first glance this is a very cool way to experience some of the most extreme of human activities, minus the actual physical risks. There is, however, another enormous potential. Since the brain cannot distinguish between what is real and what is imagined, or in this case, vividly displayed in an immersion context, we can experience all the bio-chemical responses to extreme situations. This means we can learn how to harness our emotional and mental focus at a far more enhanced rate than we have done previously.

If we consider our hyper-connected, fast-paced world, it is our key responsibility to fast-track our emotional intelligence and self-mastery if we are to handle all the pressures and far-reaching effects of leadership context. From linear 10-year business plans to human cyborgs, from fax machines to global workers, how do we lead when the world and humans are so fast-paced and amplified?

What is genuine human connection, and what can be glossed over due to technological interventions and barriers? Does technology encourage connection or deflect it? How do we develop new senses that go beyond body language when our interactions are digital and remote? How do we get our information and our intuition honed when there is so much more input?

We need first of all to get beyond the duality of thinking 'us' versus 'them'.

Since we are all more connected than ever, we need to leverage the potential of humanity's collective intellectual power. We can't have our societies fighting over borders and resources as if one group was more entitled to them than others. We see this fear of the other rising strongly in the anti-refugee campaigns and similar sentiments touted around the world. "We can't afford to help them" is a limited perspective that has a false sense of borders. What one person does affects all of us; what one group claims as their own denies the potential opportunities if we share resources.

I believe whole-heartedly that if we took a collective, world-centric approach to managing the resources on our planet, then those resources would be sufficient for all of us to live comfortably in a healthy and happy way.

> In *Abundance – The Future is Better Than you Think* (2012),[14] Peter Diamonds and Steven Kotler say: "The greatest tool we have for tackling our grand challenges is the human mind. The information and communications revolution now underway is rapidly spreading across the planet. Over the next eight years, three billion new individuals will be coming online, joining the global conversation, and contributing to the global economy. Their ideas – ideas we've never had access to – will result in new discoveries, products and inventions that will benefit us all."

The case for Abundance is compelling

As leaders we must be mindful that we are not defaulting to the fear story, the story of the 'other' as the cause of our problems. Our leadership can be an opportunity to expand perspective, knowledge, and insight.

Imagine the books written, the art cultivated, the music that could uplift, the scientific breakthroughs that could happen if we democratised internet access and learning, if we helped our fellow humans to eat well enough so they could think and learn? The opportunities for finding solutions to our intractable earth challenges are nigh, and we can unleash our collective brainpower.

We have the technological opportunity to do it, and we have a global context that demands it. What we need now is the personal resolve to act on it.

5. Risk the 'real' with *Moments*

So what is different about this book? How can we move on from the vulnerability of the 'raw' to the genuine expression of the 'real'?

Dale Carnegie in his classic 1936 book *How to Win Friends and Influence People* [15] advocated for 'be nice, get what you want'. At the time it was ground-breaking work, as it challenged the centuries-old leadership model of 'do as I command.'

When you were the 1930s boss, there was no relationship with people around you. They were there to do your bidding. Being interested in others or taking a moment to ask about them challenged the notion that the boss was above needing to be personable. The boss had power and authority; that was enough. Once the industrial age matured and pushed us into offices, the rise of the service economy saw a need for a new kind of leadership. People had more choices than they had previously. Relationships, trust, and rapport became the new currency.

Today, we have Brené Brown advocating for new kind of relationships. In her books, including *Rising Strong* (2015), [16] she espouses the power of being vulnerable and being open-hearted. She espouses that we need to be 'raw' to be seen and heard. Leaders are now not only required to be pleasant and engaging, but to share their mistakes, their fears, and their emotions. This kind of work is terrifying for most of us, as we feel we need to push again through centuries of conditioning that says to show emotion is to be weak. Brown maintains that sharing emotion is a sign of strength, not weakness, due to the courage it takes to show our inner turmoil to others.

I believe that Brown has not quite managed to reclaim the 'vulnerability' word and make it an emblem of strength. When we hear 'raw', we have the image of oozing open wounds. It sounds painful and dangerous. Vulnerability and being raw still carries a tinge of openness that is risky. At least at first glance. I think this is because there is a huge inward focus in the vulnerability narrative: it is all about declaring one's own thoughts and feelings, and hoping it lands well, or trusting that because it was said with honesty that it will be honoured.

The truth is that when people share their emotions and tremble under their weight, they are incredibly self-conscious. They are gripped and focused by their emotional waves. Releasing the dam of emotions, even if it is a measured release, is still largely a one-way affair.

There is a more evolved way to declare one's truth, and it requires advanced emotional intelligence and self-awareness.

In *Moments*, the more evolved way to express one's truth is simply to be real. This is the ability to speak our perspective and own our emotions, yet not be buffeted by them. The emotions are there, but we are not afraid of them. We are not reacting to them, we are not even controlling them – we are simply experiencing them.

Our perspective is not in trying to decipher our own story, but from a third person perspective – while at the same time being fully present. We can observe from our own eyes, experience our feelings, and still able to observe the sentiment and response of others. Speaking our truth is not a volatile or scary affair, because we are simply owning all of who we are. We are not afraid of it. We do not make excuses for it. We can even have a bit of humour about our own inner quibbles. The ability to be real is to be able to talk about ourselves and our experiences with an openness that is not reactive or risky. It means speaking our truth in full ownership of all of its likely errors and possible misguided filters.

Being 'raw' means speaking our truth with a tremor of worry about self

Being 'real' means speaking our truth with trust that no matter what, we are OK. It involves radical self-acceptance while still being open to criticism, faults, and course corrections.

The journey to becoming real is moving from the comfort of black-and-white perspectives to the disquiet of shades of grey – *and being ok with that*. Uncertainty, multiplicity, and polarities make up our perspective. The truth is always slippery, so we accept that our version of the truth is correct as it is, for the moment, given the current constraints of perception and perspective.

In being real, we own our perspective and we seek others to help us broaden our view. We know that we have filters from our social conditioning, and yet we aim to reach through these to a collaborative sense of reality. Being real means simply saying and seeing and feeling as who we are, right now, and knowing this too can change.

Moments is about helping you be more real. I want you to get through the 'raw' stage as quickly as possible so you can be centered in your personal power, relaxed in being and speaking you, as far as you know yourself.

We've got a whole lot of social conditioning to sort through as we do this.

PART TWO

Moments of Truth (Personal)

6. What is a moment of truth?

The truth-teller's guide to developing perception

Finding our perspective and developing deep presence gives us perception. Moments of truth are opportunities to dig deep to find the qualities we did not think we had. They give us the gift of perception and the ability to write an empowering narrative about the experiences we face.

> To be or not to be – that is the question:
>
> Whether 'tis nobler in the mind to suffer
>
> The slings and arrows of outrageous fortune,
>
> Or to take arms against a sea of troubles,
>
> And, by opposing, end them.
>
> Thus conscience does make cowards of us all,
>
> And thus the native hue of resolution
>
> Is sicklied o'er with the pale cast of thought,
>
> And enterprises of great pitch and moment,
>
> With this regard their currents turn awry,
>
> And lose the name of action.
>
> *– William Shakespeare, Hamlet*

Hamlet's soliloquy is an extreme case for a moment of truth: to live or not live. Our resolve is often 'sicklied over' when we allow the 'pale cast of thoughts' to intervene in our moments of truth. In other words, we talk ourselves out of taking action all the time. We get caught up in our own minds and fail to follow through. It is this, our inner voice, that is our biggest saboteur.

Moments of truth are tests of spirit. They happen when values meet choice and we choose who we are and who we will become as a result. There are three types of moments of truth:

1. **Bridging Moments.** This is when we consciously choose to align our behaviour with our values. We walk our talk.

2. **Crucible Moments.** This is an ordeal we go through that changes us forever. We make sense of the senseless.

3. **Rock Bottom Moments.** These are the times where we feel the lowest of the low. We either give up, or go on.

The inner voice that rises in moments of truth can also be our grandest ally, once we learn how to harness it. Developing our inner voice starts to give us critical perspective. When this combines with personal power, we develop resolve to carry through and take action.

Without either power or perspective, we allow the inner voice of worry to toss us about in indecision like a tiny boat on chaotic seas.

7. Bridging moments

"I'm not doing enough."

Steven runs an international educational institution. He is midway through his second contract after launching a global change initiative to shift the cultural focus of the organisation. He turned the numbers around from being a bottomless pit of debt to rising profits. He's handled internal power challenges and staff issues and fronted the media with extensive political commentary.

Not done enough.

I ask him to explain. He says: "I'm not really honouring my commitment to reduce carbon emissions and help reverse or at least stem the climate change spiral we're in. I feel like I'm doing lip service to it. It's something I believe passionately in, and yet I've done nothing substantial to affect change."

Steven can list accolades and projects and daring initiatives that would more than validate the label of a 'successful' leader. However, the pain of failing to live up to his values was palpable when he spoke of his concern for the fate of humanity and the planet. He feels a failure, in his own eyes. He feels he is letting himself down, not living his full potential, and betraying his deepest concerns. He judges himself as impotent; all talk, not enough action.

Three things here are crippling Steven:

1. **Mindset/Perception.** Unless he changes the course of the planet's environmental health, Steven feels he has failed as a leader. This is the pessimist's view. He cites Al Gore, saying "people swing from denial or ignorance to despair". Despair is not a very constructive emotion.

2. **Resolve/Action.** Until he changes his day-to-day actions and acts in integrity with his intentions, Steven feels the ache of being out of integrity.

3. **Impact.** Steven cannot change the course of the planet alone. He can, however, take action for influence to set ripples in action.

How does Steven – and how do all of us – define a life well-lived?

There is an adage that says 'show me your calendar and your bank statement and I will know immediately what you value'. This indicates clearly what your actual values are, as opposed to your aspirational ones.

The *values gap* is when we discover there is a gap between who we think we are (what we believe and what we value) and the actions we actually take. If we say we will take out the garbage, do we do it? If we say we will be there on time, are we punctual? Do we honour our wedding vows? If we value honesty, do we always speak the truth? If we cherish family, where do they sit in the hierarchy of our calendar?

Moments of truth are the choices we make when no one is watching. They are the commitments we make to ourselves to live our values. And it ain't easy! We can make all sorts of excuses when there are no witnesses. And yet, somewhere deep within our conscience, tweaks our integrity. We know on a cellular level when we are out of alignment with our best self. How do we make that commitment become our lived experience?

8. How do we cross the bridge?

When I worked at Outward Bound Australia, we ran a fabulous exercise called the 'Values Journey'. It's a literal as well as figurative journey. One of the places we ran it was in a spectacular valley full of kangaroos. The participants were given an envelope with some instructions, and directed to amble through the valley, stopping at various points for different reflection activities. The stunning surroundings (which allowed participants to be absent of mobile technology and alone with their thoughts) provided the perfect vehicle for honest self-assessment.

My private mentoring clients undertake a similar exercise in their own time.

The Values Journey looks like this:

1. Start by reviewing what you learnt about values while growing up. What did your parents and families teach you about what is important? What did they teach you about family, work, money, and life? You then explore what else you learnt from school, mentors, and friends about the same.

2. The next step is to identify the current desired values (the aspirational values). If you were being the best version of yourself, what values would you hold dear?

3. Then you rank them. And if you had to choose one out of the top three (and only one), which one would it be? Then do the same evaluation with the remaining two. This gives you your top three values.

4. There you assess the gap between your aspirational values

and the *actual* values you currently live by. For example, you might say you value 'adventure', but if you never do anything adventurous, then this is a gap: a gap between intention and action. Identifying the gaps is a huge reality check. This is where you can start to work out why your life is not measuring up to your expectations.

Then we commit to action.

What do we need to let go of to live the version of our lives based on our aspirational values? What part of our personality, habits, and faults, are we willing to abandon to be the version we aspire to be? What comes next is the hardest part: committing and following through in the day-to-day moments. It's helpful to list these on a piece of paper, then burn it symbolically.

Three strategies to help you cross the bridge over the values gap

Prepare

Mindset / Perception. Decide to be a change maker, starting with your immediate sphere of influence. This means honouring commitments you make to yourself about who you want to be and what values you want to express in the world.

Steven did this by holding the tension of wanting to make a global impact relate back to his daily actions. He now focuses on the immediate personal while at the same time thinking strategically about big-picture global issues.

Resolve / Action. Match new habits and behaviours to these values. Start small. Make every habit and action incremental to build momentum.

Steven decided to start by taking baby steps towards global influence. He does this through engaging in public conversations about global warming and blogging publicly about the need for climate action; from global to personal actions.

Impact. Measure your impact first by the effort you make in the world.

Steven acknowledges that his public position gives him a platform that many do not have. He measures his impact through honouring his own personal commitments and the amount of opportunities he takes to advance the climate change agenda.

Follow through

Outsource accountability. Tell a friend, personal trainer, accountant, or spouse about your commitment. Ask them to check in with you each week.

Steven hired me to keep his big picture objectives and his personal discipline front and center. It works!

Journal daily. When we reflect daily on our integrity and the promise we made, we renew the vows to ourselves.

Steven has a regular journal practice. It shows him where he keeps cycling old unhelpful thought patterns, as well as where his thinking and leadership have evolved.

Anchor your commitment

Put physical reminders in your environment such as post-it notes, alarms, postcards, trinkets, or screensavers.

Steven is tech savvy. He has reminders in his iPad and phone. He keeps his tablet handy so he can jot down ideas, read articles, and extend his thinking and advocacy in the smaller moments.

9. Crucible moments

Insight

"Maybe you're not meant to have children," said my oncologist, Professor Hacker (yes, my surgeon's real name). This was a narrative I was not prepared to accept.

On my 40th birthday I started bleeding, and I knew it was game over. On our last shot at IVF we had agreed to give up and move on. At that moment I knew there would be no babies for us. I lay down on the kitchen floor and howled. It was the kind of mad, ugly grief that squeezes the soul breathless and black. There were no thoughts, just a gaping chasm of pain.

It had been a long experience for us. I'd gone through cervical cancer with advanced surgery and chemotherapy a few years before. When I recovered from that I was already 37, and the proverbial clock was indeed ticking.

Once given the all-clear from the oncologist, we went straight to the IVF doctor, ready for the miracles of modern medicine. After our trauma of cancer, we were ready for some good news and happy times. Baby making was supposed to be fun after all!

Well, IVF is neither fun nor easy. We had one setback after another. Our eggs did not fertilise on their own, my cancer scars made the normal procedures difficult and required more surgery. I had a dodgy cancer screen in the middle of one round, I got hyper-stimulation of the ovaries (excess oestrogen) and had to delay, and we discovered we were both carriers of cystic fibrosis and needed genetic mapping, including getting blood samples from our respective parents (both sets still alive, but mine were in Canada). We had paperwork go missing and almost had to cancel a round of procedures at a critical last minute point (wasting time and money and eggs). And then when all seemed perfect, I got salmonella poisoning right in the middle of a critical procedure. I was seriously ill.

It had been three years of trying, multiple blood tests, screens, assessments, needles, and drugs. In one year I had been under general anaesthetic five times. We decided to give it one more chance. Then I turned 40, and our last attempt was a fail.

Lying on the kitchen floor with the sadness seeping from me, I wondered about Mother Nature, God, and Fate. It did not seem fair to me that good people like me and Rob, who would make brilliant and loving parents, would be denied the chance to do so with our own biological child. Over the coming days my emotions swung between grief, despair, and a ripple of hope. The door had closed on our future as parents. What did the other door offer us? What did a life without children look like?

It would have been very easy to take up the story that the universe was conspiring against us. It certainly seemed that way. Every part of our journey was met with ridiculous hurdles. These were pretty huge signs that things were not meant to be. Perhaps my surgeon was right. I was not meant to have children.

What then was I meant to do? What was my life about? How could I make productive sense of this mess?

Whether it's a deep personal failure like this one, or a business collapse, or a professional blunder, we can feel chasms of pain. As a leader, learning to make sense of these events is the secret to influence, first over ourselves.

About crucible moments

In their *Harvard Business Review* article "Crucibles of Leadership",[17] Warren Bennis and Robert J. Thomas say: "The crucible experience was a trial and a test, a point of deep self-reflection that forced them to question who they were and what mattered to them. It required them to examine their values, question their assumptions, hone their judgment. And, invariably, they emerged from the crucible stronger and more sure of themselves and their purpose--changed in some fundamental way."

A crucible has a double meaning. It is a vessel that is heated to great temperatures to melt metals, and also means a trial or ordeal by which a person is transformed. In my book *Composure* (2015), I looked at what it takes to guide others through a crucible experience. It's a different kettle of fish when we are immersed in it ourselves. As humans, we may unwittingly find ourselves in a crucible. These moments take three forms:

1. **Personal:** Loss, death, divorce, illness.

2. **People:** A complex and challenging mess with other people. It's a moment when we are the steward for the group, and where we need to lead a charge.

3. **Threshold:** Venturing in to the unknown, learning new skills, starting a new career, traveling to unknown lands.

No-one wishes for one of the first two – a Personal or People crucible. These are the ones that catch us off-guard and demand more of us than we know, or think ourselves capable of. The third, Threshold crucibles, are usually ones of our own choosing, and have a positive and exciting tinge of adventure to them.

To emerge through a crucible stronger and better for it, there is one essential skill needed: the ability to craft a narrative about the experience. This is the ability to make sense of the senseless and be able to craft a story about the challenges we faced, how we met them, and how we become better individuals and better leaders as a result.

How do we do that? How do we make sense of the senseless?

10. How to develop perspective – making sense of the senseless

"Every cloud has a silver lining."

"There is no failure, just feedback." – *Tony Robbins*

"I am either winning or I'm learning." – *Nelson Mandela*

In the heat of a crucible moment, these feel like trite 'pull your socks up' messages. It's a big leap to go from a shitty experience to seeing the opportunity in the shit. It is a big leap, but not impossible. There are some things in life that truly suck. Like cancer. Like failed IVF. Like mass murder. Like the death of a child. These events are simply difficult to comprehend.

What is not helpful in these moments is creating a narrative that makes us feel powerless.

The core message of 'Acceptance and Commitment Therapy' is to accept what is out of your control, then commit to taking action that improves and enriches your life. Stephen Covey also talks about this principle in the *The 7 Habits of Highly Effective People* (1989).[18] He encourages us to focus on our sphere of control and our sphere of influence, rather than get obsessed with our sphere of concern. The sphere of concern often holds elements that are outside of our ability to impact. To focus on them makes us feel powerless and small – it's better to focus on what we can control, like our thoughts and actions.

To develop perspective there are three critical steps:

1. Make sense of now
2. Make sense of the past
3. Make sense of the future.

Make sense of now

Through acceptance, you embrace completely the stark reality of your current circumstances. You accept that now is a terrible moment, and that you're fully in that moment. It also means owning up to what you've contributed to the situation (without beating yourself up).

Feel the feelings you have, fully. This doesn't have to be a full-blown emotional firehose! This is what people most fear when it comes to emotions – that they will lose control, and be drawn in to a deep cesspit of choking energy. Just notice how you feel, pay attention to it, and accept it as your experience in this moment.

Decide to feel better. Little moment by little moment, gently guide your focus to better feeling thoughts. Seek relief and hope in your perspective.

— ▢ —

On the day I truly knew I would never be a mother, I experienced deep despair. I would never have my own biological children. I would never be pregnant. I would never have maternity leave and make friends with other mums from playgroup. I would never teach my child about the beauty of the world and all its glorious magic. I would never teach my child how to drive, or hold them close when they needed comforting, or wait up for them if they were up late, or share outdoor adventures, or watch them get married and have children of their own. I would never be a grandmother. There was a finite line under my biological future and family tree.

It felt bad. Really bad.

For about three minutes.

Then I felt better.

I would never have to change diapers. Or have sleepless nights. Or deal with embarrassing two-year-old tantrums. Or spend Saturdays in the rain watching endless sporting events. Or deal with vomit. Or whining. Or endless doctor/dentist/school bills for the next 20 years.

I felt relief. Then I felt guilt for feeling relief.

We're supposed to want to have kids. We're supposed to be devastated if it doesn't turn out that way. We're supposed to feel an emptiness if we don't have kids. But I didn't. I felt OK. In fact, I was happy and excited about what my life could look like, now that we weren't in the eternal waiting room of "will it happen or not?"

And I was OK with feeling OK about not having kids.

Make sense of the past

There is a helpful exercise to help you see patterns in your life, and to choose good feeling thoughts about them.

I encourage my coaching clients to draw their life in mountain peaks and deep valleys. You simply draw a mountain range then plot the high and the low points as you remember. Look at the points and ask of each one: What happened?

- · How did you feel?
- · What have you made that has meaning in your life?
- · What did you learn about yourself, life, relationships, work, and other themes through those experiences?
- · What are some common themes?
- · What great insight can you pass on to others through your lived experience?

I have done this exercise and mapped a lot of peaks and troughs in my life. Looking at the picture, I realised I am a very stubborn person. I am relentless in my objectives and ruthless to the point of self-sacrifice towards my goals. This pattern was repeated through my IVF experience: bloody-minded determination kept us crawling over the hurdles that fate dealt us. Thinking on it, I felt that perhaps self-sacrifice had its limits, and that maybe a gentler future might be in order.

The sense I made of my past gave me a sense of what my future might look like instead: gentle, free, fun.

Make sense of the future

Once you have reflected on the peaks and troughs of your life experience, decide that you want something different for your future. Choose to take the lessons of past experiences and apply them to your next steps. Identify how you want your life to be like, to feel like, and how you'd like to experience your life from day to day.

— ◻ —

What did this look like, through my IVF crucible? I decided to be happy. I decided to live life fully and to take advantage of what a life without parental duties afforded: yearly international travel, renovating our house, growing my business. I actively sought out the positive benefits of a life without children, and started to delight in the freedom and possibilities.

It's not the life I thought I'd end up living, but hot damn, it's good!

This process is about pivoting your perspective

In finding sense where none is immediately apparent, we decide to make something meaningful from a crappy situation. We can look at our trials as part of the Hero's Journey, and seek a lesson or insight. In the Hero's Journey, according to mythologist Joseph Campbell,[19] the hero faces many trails and challenges. By vanquishing monsters, demons, and dragons, he or she gains new insight that is valuable on their journey.

When we are immersed in a crucible moment not of our own making, however, it is difficult to reach for the lesson or insight when all we feel is the murkiness of the struggle. Through deliberate practice and focus, we can pivot away from the darkness towards a more useful frame.

When I was going through chemotherapy for cervical cancer, I asked myself many questions to find the meaning in the disease. The first answers were not that helpful: "I'm a failure, it's my fault, I didn't manage myself or my mindset well enough, I'm not meant to have babies." Sitting with the blackness of self-blame, this eventually subsided and I managed to do an expanded pivot.

When we pivot in this way, this lifts us out of the quagmire of negativity. When we ask "How could this serve others?," our attachment to our own drama falls away and we are focused on contribution.

As I trudged through the mud of cancer, I resolved to make my experience one of insight for me and for others. I blogged about my experience. These insights were largely about discovering the beauty in small moments, of shrinking focus to faith and not fear regardless of potential circumstances, and to living each day as a gift. Thriving after cancer became my beacon, and helped light my path. From the feedback I had from readers, it helped them to deal with their own personal crisis, or that of a loved one.

I have pivoted in the same way with my IVF journey. I resolved to make my life beautiful. I would live a deep and meaningful life full of experiences that deepen my connection to self, to others, and this miraculous planet. I see it as a sacred contract to make the most of my one beautiful life. In doing so, I intend to light a path for others so that we may journey in happiness and discovery, no matter our circumstances.

Insight

"What am I doing here?" I sobbed. I was lying face-down in the mud with a 40kg canoe pinning me down awkwardly between slippery logs. I was 16, and somewhere in Northwest Ontario on a portage to carry canoes from one lake to another. The other girls on the trip had gone ahead and I was left to carry one of the canoes. Again.

It was raining. Nothing unusual about that. It had been raining for weeks, and we were now used to the uncomfortable dampness of our clothes and the shivering when we stopped paddling for too long. So I lay in the mud, feeling the trickle of rain from my jacket soak a little more into my thermals. I could smell the moss and the mud like an earthy coffee. I wriggled a little, trying to budge the canoe. No luck; it was jammed.

I was seriously angry. I was angry with the others for leaving me behind, I was angry that I had to carry the canoe again, and I was angry that I was stuck under the stupid canoe. Life sucked. I just wanted to be warm, dry, and somewhere else. Anywhere but here.

I realised it was going to be at least an hour before anyone came back for the rest of the gear. That meant another hour trapped, breathing muddy forest floor. That made me cry and swear even more.

Then I became truly enraged. With all the strength I could muster, I hauled myself to my knees with the 40kg canoe grinding between trees as I swore and panted and jammed it upwards. It worked! I was free. I swore a little more, heaving from the effort, and kicked the canoe viciously. "Bastard!" I yelled. I knew no-one could hear me. It would keep the bears away though.

Once I had gathered myself a little, I knew it was time to get going. There was no point waiting, as I knew the others would not find it any easier than I had. I was on my own.

So I got back under the canoe, slipped the yoke onto my shoulders, and with some more swearing, wrenched the canoe from its hold between the trees. I seesawed back and forth, and got it facing the right direction, up the muddy, slippery slope. We were away, me and the bastard canoe.

After I met up with the group again, the rest of the day was more of the same: paddle a bit, haul the gear around the rapids, across overgrown narrow muddy trails, load up and shove off, while the rain streamed, oblivious to our bitter moods.

Later that night, after we'd set up camp and stood hovering around the fire, steaming as the rain had eased little, we held the usual debrief of the day. I was still seething from the gristle of my thoughts, feeling hard done by, always carrying the canoe. So I said so. I said I thought it would be a good idea if we shared the canoe carrying a little more.

Feeling smug that I had finally put this injustice on the table, I waited. One of the leaders, Gill, finally spoke.

"Zoë, not everybody is as strong as you. Some people are just built differently. On a canoe trip we all put in as much as our ability allows."

I felt the realisation and then the shame wash over me. Three of the girls were much shorter than me, and not that big. They would be carrying almost their full body weight if they took on a canoe. It would be a serious injury risk if they attempted it. I was mortified I had not considered this previously, and I felt my heart race and my face burn red.

"I'm sorry. I never thought about it like that before."

Some of them offered to try harder the next day, which only made me feel worse. I had pointed out their physical 'weakness' in a very aggressive way, as they bravely tried to bridge the judgment cast upon them.

I learned much over that incident. First, looking back to the effort of getting up out of the mud, I had surprised myself with my strength and determination. I discovered what grit really was: the teeth gnashing, single-minded perseverance to make it through a crappy situation. The second, most important lesson was expanding my perspective to consider the full context. I had been seeing the world through my own narrow lens (albeit one stuck in a world of pain and mud), and had failed to be considerate of others and how they might be suffering too. It's hard to feel you can't pull your weight, so to speak, due to your physical limitations. I discovered empathy and compassion.

I took this key lesson, 'each according to their own ability', as a key leadership principle on all of my future wilderness expeditions. At Outward Bound Australia, this was especially important with young boys' groups. The difference in their development was often extreme, with some boys aged 12 still with a child's body, while others had had a growth surge and towered over their peers and teachers. 'Each according to their own ability' was an important mantra to diffuse any sense of superiority in one camp, and inadequacy in the other. Learning to help each other, and to find diverse ways people contribute to a group effort – not always physically – was a crucial team leadership insight.

Crucibles help reveal strengths of character. We are stronger than we think we are. I've had few people say to me: "You're so brave, going through what you did with cancer/IVF/wilderness journeys". What they are really saying is: "I don't want to experience what you've experienced. It sounds way too painful and uncomfortable."

We don't often choose crucibles; they choose us. We would not often pick someone else's crucible, not wanting to experience they have had: for example we would not pick to be an amputee, or to go through a devastating family loss. All these people are humans like us, and they have found remarkable strengths. The crucible burned away any option of weakness, and left only resolve.

We don't have to wonder whether we would be up to it, however. We can actually build inner resolve and resilience that can prepare us for the crucibles we choose – like a new job, or moving to another country – as well as the ones we would not want, like disease or loss.

11. How to develop the key capacities to handle a crucible experience

If we do find ourselves in deep in the crucible with the fire raging, there is one key capacity that will help us realise that we are indeed cut out for whatever is sent our way.

Let feelings be teachers

We've got to wrestle with the blackest of emotions, from fear, to shame, to despair. If we can sit in the storm of these, and just let them wash through us without holding on tight, then we will be able to let the feelings go. We won't be paralysed from the fear of feeling bad. We'll feel bad for a bit, then we feel better.

I wrote extensively about this technique in *Composure*. The essence of the technique of sitting in the storm of feelings is observing feelings in the body. By becoming aware of the energy that is building and gripping in the body, we give it a pathway for release. The act of observation acts as a pressure valve.

Through observing, we embrace the fullness of our emotions and experience them without needing to act (or react) on them. This way, we don't make any of our emotions go 'bad'. We may have vengeful thoughts and feelings, but we don't need to act on them. We simply acknowledge them, observe them, and watch them fade as we draw our attention back to who we are and how we want to show up in the world.

Feelings are great teachers. They are a gift to us. They help us explore a bigger version of ourselves. Hate, for example, can be a huge powerful liberator. It needs us to be totally present to it so we can then inquire gently, "What is beneath the hate? What is really going on for me here? What is this feeling trying to show me *about myself*?"

These so-called 'negative' emotions, the ones we are most afraid of and often try to suppress, are huge opportunities for insight and personal growth.

This is how we can experience hate being transformed into love. I first learned this process from Jason Irving. He is my long-time spiritual advisor and healer, and his work has helped me become centered and happy.

We feel hate as an intense bitterness burning within. If we feel hate fully, we can ask, "what does hate show me about myself?" Hate, at its center, is not really about other people. It's about the stories we have told ourselves about them and our relationship to them.

In a workshop with Jason, I witnessed a young woman identify hate for a man who had abused her many times over many years. Hatred had become her burning shield of defence. As she felt this feeling and asked "what is going on for me with this feeling?" she realised the hatred she was experiencing was really towards herself. She had allowed the experience of the abuse to define her, to keep her scared and small, and to run a narrative inside that said "I deserve to be abused."

When she had that insight, she realised that her abuser was not holding her prisoner; she was. Her hatred turned to anger. Again, she asked, "what is this anger showing me about myself?" She realised it was anger towards herself for carrying the burden of self-punishment for so long.

With the realisation that she was doing this to herself, she now knew she was in control of her emotions and her own narrative. She realised she had constructed stories about who she was, and what she derived out of these repeated intense experiences. And then she realised she could form new stories about herself that were far more empowering.

Her anger turned to passion. She could create something new in her life. She could be, think, feel, and live differently.

Her passion eased into creativity. She started to entertain what was possible for herself and her life.

Creativity turned into action. The energy turned direct and focus started to run within her.

Her action turned to satisfaction, fulfilment, and love. As she experienced the fullness of who she was and what she could create in her life, she felt a boundless sense of peace and love – for herself, for her life, and for all things.

This process took just a few minutes. We could see the shifts in her body as her previously hunched shoulders relaxed, the tension in her face eased, and the light of a smile spread across her face. Jason asked her, "How do you feel?" She responded: "I feel free."

All in the group were moved deeply by her courage to simply be with her feelings, dissolve the old story constructs, and embrace a new way of being.

A key thing to mention here is that her acceptance of feelings does not mean condoning abusive behaviour. Nor does the above example in any way blame the victim for the actions of the abuser. The abuser still did vicious and horrible things, and should be held accountable for his actions. The point about this example is that she felt she was still being abused emotionally and mentally, even though he was gone. She did not need to feel this way anymore. She had a choice to be free from the past and all the feelings that had kept her feeling small and horrid.

And don't we do this too, with our own past experiences?

We all have experiences that feel bad. Maybe someone once told us: "You'll never amount to anything." And it hurt us to the quick. Our brain connected that feeling to a story it made up about who we are such as, "You're not good enough." And then our default programming started to happen. We started to look for reinforcement of that message in the events of our lives, reinforcing the belief subconsciously. Over and over we had experiences that we linked to the story of "I'm not good enough" until it ultimately held us prisoner.

With a willingness to sit on our feelings and explore them, we can dissolve those old patterns, those old links between heart and mind, until all we have left is a loving heart. And we can create new powerful links that hold us strong and beautiful.

This is how we do that:

Feel it. Notice the feeling you are experiencing, positive or negative.

Accept it. Don't try and avoid it, just accept the feeling without judgement.

Ask it. Ask what the feeling is showing you about yourself and your stories, in that moment.

12. Rock bottom moments

Turia Pitt is a remarkable example of how to survive rock bottom. She has a double degree with honours in Mining Engineering and Science. Smart and gorgeous, she worked as a model before taking up an engineering job with Rio Tinto at the Argyle Diamond Mine in Western Australia. In September 2011, Turia was trapped by a grassfire in a 100km ultra-marathon in the remote Kimberley region. She suffered burns to 65 per cent of her body, and had four fingers from her left hand and her right thumb amputated.[20]

Turia was placed in an induced coma for a month to deal with the excruciating pain. Since the fire, she has had over 200 procedures, including plastic surgery and reconstruction of her nose from bone on her forehead. In her long recovery, she had to learn how to walk, talk, and feed herself again. For two years, she wore a mask over her face to aid in the rehabilitation process.

The doctor who treated her said he had never seen anyone burned so badly survive a fire.

Now Turia has written a book, *Everything to Live For* (2013),[21] works on the Haapi Foundation (a foundation that provides kids in developing countries with the best educational resources possible), is the ambassador for Interplast (an international humanitarian organisation that provides free reconstructive surgery in developing countries), and travels the world as an inspirational speaker.

I think what makes Turia's story so compelling is that we can't imagine ourselves having that kind of focus and positivity. The thought of having our lives shattered in that way and our looks destroyed, is something none of us would sign up for. We feel guiltily grateful that it was her and not us.

This is what Turia is trying to convey in her book and public speaking. You don't know what you have inside, and it is likely you're just as ferocious as she is when you have everything to live for. For Turia, this was a loving partner and the desire to move again, to swim in the sea, and to simply enjoy life. She found meaning in her ordeal. At the end of *Everything to Live For*, she writes:

"I want to gain my doctorate in engineering and go back to work in mining. I want to become an endurance athlete: I want to run another ultra marathon; I want to compete in an Ironman. I am dedicated to raising awareness for skin donation and I would like to see a burns rehabilitation center… I have so much to do…you might say I have gone from the despair of not wanting to live to having everything to live for."

Five years after the fire, she ran her first Iron Man triathlon: 3.86km (2.4 miles) swim, 180.25 km bike ride (112 miles), and a full marathon 42.2km (26.22 miles) in Hawaii.

Turia has an iron will and a focused sense of exploring her limits.

Before the fire, she was already quite 'sporty'. But it takes more than being sporty to sign up for a 100km ultra marathon in the Kimberley desert! That is true grit material. It means exploring the boundaries of physical resilience time and time again. Of pushing the limits and the boundaries a bit more each day, each week. Not many of us have that kind of desire or tenacity to push our physical limits in that way. We content ourselves with a more comfortable life. There seems little reward from the outside for this kind of extreme limit pushing.

I firmly believe that this kind of disciplined 'tough stuff' exploration saved Turia's life. It is what kept her alive through the literal crucible of a bushfire in a gorge.

How can we work on our capacity for true grit on our own terms?

Even being an endurance athlete did not prevent Turia from reaching rock bottom. When she saw her burned face for the first time, several weeks after the incident, she was inconsolable. She had many moments when grief and despair threatened to consume her for good. She went through episodes of wanting to die rather than endure the pain of recovery and face the world with a scarred face and body.

How do you go from wanting to die from despair to an international stage where all eyes are upon you?

You don't need to be an endurance athlete. Eckhart Tolle was a German language teacher who suffered from depression. After a sleepless night he experienced a profound epiphany about the nature of the mind. He dropped out of his university studies and for two years sat on park benches around London. Now he is a speaker, author, and luminary who is recognised around the world.[22]

The 2003 fires in Canberra killed four people and destroyed over 500 homes. I met with several people who were directly affected. At the time I was working at Outward Bound, where one organisation had booked a weekend of team-building to help their people re-focus and recover after the trauma.

One woman had lost everything. Her family had piled all their worldly possessions into their car as the fire loomed and tore through their street. They'd waited just too long to escape, and as they left their house to get in the car, the garage roof collapsed and their car and all its contents were destroyed. They managed to escape to safety. Speaking of it at that weekend retreat, she laughed. She was wearing ill-fitting clothes donated from the refuge. She said, "We lost everything, but we have our lives. It's just stuff, after all."

Another woman had a completely different response. She too had lost everything, and escaped with her family safe and sound. Three years afterwards she was still traumatised, and receiving counselling for the grief of losing her family heirlooms and the near-miss they experienced.

What makes one woman laugh off a brush with death and another plummet to rock bottom? It comes down to storytelling. Our internal voice creates and governs our perspective. It determines whether what we experience is a treasure or a terror.

13. How to deal with rock bottom moments

Author J.K. Rowling once said, "Rock bottom became the solid foundation on which I rebuilt my life." As a single mother, she sat destitute in a coffee shop and wrote a story to while away the despair. We all know how that turned out.[23]

Having found rock bottom, what then?

Rowling did not go from destitute single mother to billionaire overnight. Pitt did not go from crippled burns victim to elite sportswoman and speaker in a day. Tolle did not move off the park bench to international spirituality teacher one week later.

Each of these rock bottom moments has a few key elements in common.

What we really need to let go of at rock bottom is our own self-critical voice. When we let this voice drift away, we can hear the deeply resonant one that resides within. This is the deep voice of true awareness, of pure appreciation, of exquisite love of all life and living. We let go of the stories of disappointment and of shame, and we look with new eyes upon a world that is rich and ever present with joy and beauty. Losing everything we thought was important is the gift. We discover everything we ever wanted was always there, to be experienced now.

Rowling found it in her creative outlet of writing. Pitt discovered this in her new sense of purpose. Tolle experienced this as a deep abiding peace. Each had to let go of something first before they could lift off rock bottom.

What do we need to sacrifice to leave rock bottom?

We might need to leave vanity, shame, pride, and destructive habits behind. Pitt let go of her old identity and face; all her expectations of what might have been to be buried. Regret, remorse, despair and all emotions that are backwards-facing need to be let go.

We might need to discover help, connection, compassion, self-acceptance, self-love, health, faith, and love. All this requires a pivot of focus. Before you see the silver lining, you need to accept the cloud. In this light, a bounce at rock bottom requires: letting go of what might have been and what was; acceptance of what is; and focus on what is possible.

Helpful frames to pivot at rock bottom

Letting Go Thoughts

- What does hanging onto this negative emotion keeping me from doing?
- What might my life look like without these thoughts?
- What am I prepared to let go of in order to be free?

Acceptance Thoughts

- This too shall pass.
- When you have nothing, you have nothing to lose.
- Being uncomfortable is OK.
- When I have nothing, I still have a choice: I can choose how to think, how to feel, what I focus on. I can choose fear or faith – it's up to me.

What Is Possible Thoughts

- The only way out is up.
- What is there in my life that I can appreciate?
- What is there in my life I can be grateful for?

- What can I learn from this?
- What might be good about this?
- What one thing can I do about this?
- What do I want instead?

Decide to be a victor instead of a victim. When we experience regret, remorse, guilt, or despair, we cling to something beyond our reach, outside of our control. Taking responsibility for all the results in one's life can be confronting. And empowering. We discover we're in charge! We get to choose how things work out.

From pivot to power

After my cancer surgery I could barely take one step from the bed to the chair. Seven months later, I ran my sixth marathon. Turia Pitt could not feed herself or touch her face for months after her surgery. Now she has completed an Ironman in Hawaii. When we look forward from our state of struggle it is impossible to imagine such leaps happening immediately. The important thing is to hold the image of what is possible, then get back to the work of one tiny step at a time.

It's the focus on meaningful progress that gives momentum

When we make meaningful progress *visible*, then we create accountability.[24] Pitt wanted to spend her first Christmas after the fire out of hospital at her brother's apartment, just to get a sense of normal. He lived in tall building without an elevator, so she needed to be able to get in and out of the car and climb seven flights of stairs. Every day she climbed the stairs at the hospital, each day going a little further than the day before, until she could climb all seven flights. She made it to her brother's for Christmas. The stairs were both visible and meaningful. They anchored her to a tangible sense of progress and kept her from falling into despair. As long as there was progress, she had something to galvanise focus and action.

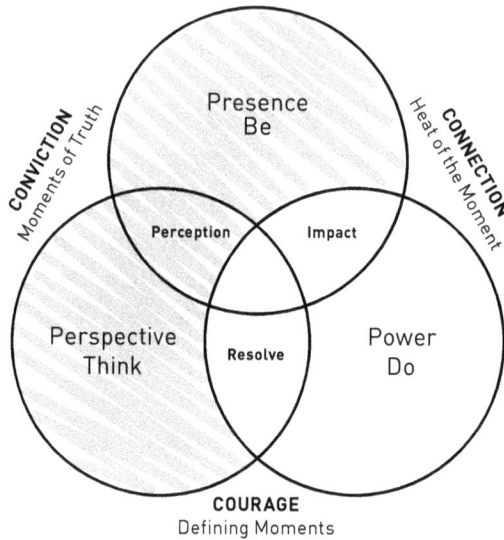

Key takeaways

Gaining perspective and developing deep presence gives us perception

Moments of truth are an opportunity to dig deep to find the qualities we did not think we had. As we forge *presence* and *perspective*, our *perception* of what is possible deepens. And it is in this perception we develop *conviction* about the right path forward.

Bridging our 'values gap' requires daily commitment and reflection to live by the values we choose

Developing perspective helps make sense of the senseless or of crucible moments

We do this by making sense of now, our past, and future. We create stories about what happens to us that give us a sense of power and autonomy. We need to develop personal power in order to cope with the crucible moments we do not choose for ourselves. We do this by letting feelings be our teachers.

To bounce at rock bottom, we need to:

- Let go of what might have been and what was
- Accept what is
- Focus on what is possible
- Make progress meaningful and visible.

Being seen, heard, and valued by others begins first with ourselves. We need to see and hear ourselves deeply to value the gifts we bring to the world.

PART THREE

Defining Moments (Ethical)

14. About defining moments

The truth-teller's guide to developing resolve

Exploring turning points and using those 'finger on the button' moments helps us develop courage. These are 'do or die' moments. We learn how to make choices on the edge. There is risk of backlash, as well as opportunity. In defining moments, we need to hone our perspective and our power for our resolve to take action.

There are a few types of defining moments:

· Challenges to leadership

· Challenges to values

· 'Rock and a hard place' moments

· Speaking up.

Challenges to leadership happen when everything is on the line: reputation, success of the project or organisation, and support of the team. If we make the wrong move the jig is up, and the consequences – both personally and professionally – are dire. Challenges to our values happen when we are confronted with the choice to either bow down or stand up for our convictions. There is risk both ways.

'Rock and hard place' moments are ethical challenges, when each choice feels difficult and fraught with peril. How do we choose the right path without going down in flames? And speaking up is laced with risk: we risk challenging authority and all the vindictive repercussions that may entail. We risk the disapproval of our colleagues who feel the threat to the status quo. We also risk the inner corrosion that comes from not living our values, and the guilt of complacency.

We handle these moments by expanding our perspective and honing our power.

Perspective considers: "what is best for the greater good and the greater number in this situation?"

Power comes from moving beyond ego to a higher definition of ourselves as leaders: our responsibility and impact on other human beings and the world around us.

When perspective and power combine, we ignite our resolve and the courage to handle the trickiest of situations.

15. When leadership is challenged

Insight

He sat on the bus alone, waiting, for an hour. Eventually, he realised no one was coming. As the new MD and COO, Nigel had found that first day rough, and there were many sour faces in the crowd. He figured change was always a hard pill to swallow, and what he was proposing was radical change. A clean sweep of the staffing decks with major job losses. The company was bleeding market share and profitability. The board had stubbornly refused to address the warning signals, and now it was looking at the yawning chasm of irrelevance and insolvency.

Big change was needed, and it wasn't going to be fun, or pretty, or easy. But it was necessary, or none of them would have a future. On the first day as their new leader, Nigel laid it out cold for them. No point in clouding the issue with sentiment. Better to be straight up.

When he'd said at the end of the day: "Be on the bus at 7.30pm to go to dinner", he expected them to be there. At least out of obedience and duty.

No one showed. Clearly, he had a problem.

That night he rang his mentor and told her the story. His mentor told him to pour himself a glass of something strong and get ready for a long night. It was going to take a while to get the strategy together to salvage anything out of this mutiny.

Nigel stayed awake long into the night. By morning he was ready. He met his team for day two of the retreat. They were cold and steely-eyed. He ate some humble pie, and apologised. He apologised for his bravado, his brusqueness, his one-way dictatorial approach. He told them he had spent most of the night on the phone with his mentor, raking over the wounds of his failed leadership address. He proposed that they try again, with a clean slate, and that this time he would listen, he would ask questions first, and invite perspective.

They didn't jump up and hug him, nor was there cheering. Anger simmered, and the tension was strung tight like a steel wire ready to snap. Nigel invited the leadership team to speak one by one, and to give their perspective. Some voices were angry, some hurt, some suspicious. Nigel sat in the quagmire of the mess and listened, and asked questions, and asked again.

Then something remarkable started to happen. Little-by-little, the anger and frustration seeped away. They were exhausted. But slowly they started to piece together the shape of a workable plan to turn the company around.

Nigel lists this as the defining moment of his leadership history. His perspective on leadership, on his leadership in particular, changed forever in that moment. He realises it took a massive slap in the ego to stare down the truth: a leader does not lead alone. There is no leadership without others. Nigel learned that though he had authority, this did not deliver respect. Coercion is one tool of influence, but not one of the best. He learned that only in opening his perspective and developing his personal power would he have the resolve and courage to get through the confronting retreat with his reputation and job intact.

What does it take to handle a mutiny and turn it around?

16. Perspectives that help with defining moments

Multiple truths

Our own perspective is but one perspective. It is the truth as we see it, but it is not the only truth. To develop buy-in and to fully understand all aspects of an issue, we need to consider multiple truths.

Nigel's plan for turning the company around may have been the best cause of action, but it failed to consider the concerns and truths of the key stakeholders. It was a one-way directive. Buy-in needs collaborative conversations. Showing up deeply present is a start. Listening and asking questions is the best way to elicit the multiple truths that exist.

There is a difference between hard truth and brutal truth

Delivering hard truths is an important aspect of leadership. There are ways of stating the truth that do not cause a fear-based reaction. Done badly, brutal truths are 'poo bombs'. You may be speaking the truth, but it hits people in a spray that gets all over everyone, including you. Done well, hard truths are aired but invite collaborative effort. We can do this by softening the delivery. Start phrases with a confession and an invitation like, "I'm afraid to share this. It has big repercussions for us. I'm sure that together we can work it out. Here it is..."

Always consider the audience: What stage of leadership development are they at? What are their primary concerns? How might this truth affect them? Will it cause a survival-based reaction? How might they interpret the message?

Ask how you might frame the truth in a way that reassures or invites collaboration to find a way forward together.

I versus we

If we take the hero approach, we might find ourselves out in front with no-one around. Or, like Nigel, alone on the bus. Taking the hero approach means charging in like the cavalry to save the day. Without any previous relationship or history with the others, this smacks of arrogance and ego. Taking a 'we' approach means listening first, encouraging discussion, and coming to solutions together. A cavalier attitude towards the people involved will only lead to resentment and anger. In the end, the strategy or solution may not change from what you suggested, but the approach you take builds support and inclusion.

Insight

In the fabulous movie Kon-Tiki (2012), the perils of defining moments are acted out where it matters most: in life and death situations.

Thor Heyerdahl is the leader of a crazy 1947 expedition that set out to prove it was Peruvians who likely settled Polynesia by floating on rafts using ocean currents. Thor and five others build a balsam wood raft with a small hut above it, using the same materials used by the fabled Polynesian leader, Tiki. The raft had no steering capabilities, and simply trusted to the currents to float them 4,300 nautical miles, some 7,963 km, in 101 days. Nuts.

One of the crew is an engineer who is haunted by the comments of a sailor who warned the logs would bounce together, over and over, until they split the raft apart. The engineer, crippled by his fear, confronts Thor. He begs him to use the two rolls of steel wire he'd snuck aboard the raft for an extra bit of modern protection. Thor stares into his crewmate's eyes, feeling the full weight of what is being said, and what is also unsaid. His engineer does not trust the expedition, and doubts they will make it. We become aware that this kind of corrosive fear could wipe out the rest of the crew's confidence. A raft in the ocean with six men is a small place, month after month.

Thor takes the steel wire and hurls it in to the sea. The engineer collapses in despair. There is no safety left: they have no option but to believe in the idea of the raft, that they could repeat what the legend Tiki had done. Failure was not an option.

Thor's actions convey that they will make it, that his decisions are sound, and they need to hold the faith. This is the same refrain he reassures them with throughout the voyage, even when their first 20 days had them off course and facing certain death in 9-metre waves along the drift line.

On his own, the camera shows anxiety and doubt creep in to Thor's face. Had he done the right thing? Did he indeed throw away their last vestige of hope and chance of success? His fear would do nothing to encourage the crew. Later, the engineer slips overboard in shark-infested waters. Another crew member jumps in and swims out with a rescue-line and they are towed to safety.

In a quiet moment with the engineer Thor admits, "I could not save you. I cannot swim." The engineer replies, "I know. We all do."

What's revealing about these two scenes is how Thor expresses his vulnerability. He refuses to show fear and doubt because it would only serve as a corrosive element with the crew. When he admits his weakness as a leader, in his inability to swim, he discloses a weakness that is also a strength. It takes profound courage to float on a raft at the mercy of the elements without even the ability to save himself.

Both these moments are defining moments for Thor and for the rest of the crew. Thor's courage and conviction holds them together in the face of insurmountable odds. They believed in his vision because they believed in him.

Leadership in defining moments

Nigel and Thor faced similar leadership challenges: mutiny and doubt. They both dealt with it differently through carefully-honed personal power and perspective.

John C. Maxwell says, "People buy into the leader before they buy into the vision."[25] This was the issue for Nigel. He assumed his team would see the direction clearly and that would be enough to persuade them. They saw nothing of the man's character except bold arrogance.

When he apologised and invited conversation, they saw his capacity for humility and compassion. This fanned the dying embers of respect and slowly they were able to work with him instead of against him.

For Thor, his team bought into his vision when they realised his deep courage. Only a man of real conviction would risk his life as a non-swimmer on a flimsy raft in the middle of the Pacific Ocean. They figured he had the mettle to bet his life on his beliefs, and they agreed to follow him.

Both needed a deep well of personal power to handle the fear and anger of their followers in such dire circumstances. They found the courage to stay the course, even when all seemed bleak. For Nigel, this meant swallowing his pride and starting over, for his sake and the sake of the organisation's future. For Thor, this was a test of his conviction: either his theory was right, or they would all die. Thor's power was about his idea and place in history, as well as the safety of the men in his care.

Perspective kept them anchored to the bigger picture.

For Nigel, he learned that his one perspective was limited. Once he invited other perspectives, he started to build a sense of team. For Thor, the question he held on the showdown over the wire was: "What is best for the team in this moment?" He realised that the security of modern wire would actually be more dangerous for the team. This had to be a 'do or die' moment or their doubt would corrupt their conviction. It is the 'burn the boats' moment.

Hernán Cortés, the Spanish commander during the 1519 conquest of Mexico, ordered his ships to be scuttled. His men had no choice but to conquer or die. Likewise, when Thor threw the wire to the sea, he threw down the gauntlet: we do this or we die.

17. When values are challenged

On 9th October 2012, 15-year-old Malala Yousafzai boarded a bus to go to school in Swat, a northwest district of Pakistan. A gunman stopped the bus, asked for her by name, and fired at point blank range. One bullet went through the left side of Malala's forehead, travelled under her skin, and landed in her shoulder. The other bullets hit two other girls in the bus, in the hand and shoulders. Both survived. Malala was airlifted to Birmingham in England for recovery. She too survived.[26]

How does a 15-year-old girl become target of the Taliban? Where Malala lived, her father was an outspoken schoolteacher who advocated for the rights of girls, and children in general, to an education. When the Taliban moved in to the Swat region and shut down schools, he protested to the media and in public meetings. He encouraged his daughter to speak up for what she believed in. At the age of 12, Malala wrote an online diary under a pseudonym for the BBC Urdu site about her life under the Taliban, how afraid she was, and how much she wanted to go to school and get an education.

Malala also gave many interviews about the Taliban and politics in Pakistan. She knew there were risks, she knew the Taliban were deadly, but she never thought she would be a focus. She was just a girl. Malala's father was named as a target for the Taliban. They took precautions, changed routines. Yet he never thought they would go after his daughter.

After the shooting, Malala went on to speak publicly about her experience. She met Queen Elizabeth II in Buckingham Palace, and on 12th July 2013 she spoke at the United Nations to call for worldwide access to education. Not a year had passed since the attack.

In her speech she says: "The terrorists thought they would change my aims and stop my ambitions, but nothing changed in my life except this: weakness, fear and hopelessness died. Strength, power and courage was born... I am not against anyone, neither am I here to speak in terms of personal revenge against the Taliban or any other terrorist group. I'm here to speak up for the right of education for every child. I want education for the sons and daughters of the Taliban and all terrorists and extremists."

In 2014 Malala was named as the co-recipient of Nobel Peace Prize for her struggle against the suppression of children and young people, and for the right of all children to education. At 17, she is the youngest Nobel Laureate. Malala shared the prize with Kailash Satyarthi, a children's rights activist from India. She has continued her activism and now philanthropy. In 2015, at the age of 18, she opened a school for Syrian refugees in the Bekaa Valley, Lebanon, near the Syrian border. This was done through the Malala Fund she established with her father.

Malala's story tells us much about what is possible with courage and conviction. There is much that is remarkable about Malala: her burning passion for education, her courage to speak about her experiences, her tenacity and vision to advocate for that which is denied to others.

For me the most remarkable aspect of her story is the clarity of her compassion. "I am not against anyone... I want education for the sons and daughters of the Taliban and all terrorists and extremists." The love that radiates from that simple statement, by someone who had been shot in the head with the intention to kill her, is heart-expanding.

If we could guide all our leadership with that kind of love and compassion, we would end so many troubles, and build so many beautiful futures.

– □ –

A note on martyrs

I always thought martyrs were crazy. I mean, who would give up their life for the sake of an idea?

Take Thomas More for example. King Henry VIII was his best mate. That is until Henry decided that he needed to take over control over the Church, ostensibly to make the rules of marriage and divorce in his favour, and endorse his second marriage to Anne Boleyn. It wasn't the only reason. As head of the Church of England, Henry would became absolute ruler of his domain, in spiritual matters as well as all things kingly and judicial. Power-monger might be another term for it.

Thomas More had an issue with that. Being a devout Catholic and a lawyer, it was sacrilege for anyone to put themselves above the Pope, or replace the Pope as representative of God on earth. More then refused to take the oath declaring the King as the supreme Head of the Church in England.

As Henry did not want to kill off his lifelong mentor and friend, More was imprisoned for a year. But Henry really needed him to stump up and take the oath, rather than be seen as tolerating a decrier. So More was sentenced to beheading, and off came his head.

I always thought this was crazy. More sacrificed his life, and left his family of four children to their own fate for the sake of his principles.

I have the same thought about other martyrs through the ages. Japanese *kamikaze* fighter pilots ramming their planes into allied targets for the glory of Japan. Joan of Arc dying at the stake for France. And contemporary jihadists blowing themselves up to rid the world of infidels and advance their version of Islam.

As I said, it sounds nuts.

Knowing Malala's story now, it does not seem so foolish to stand up for what you believe. Education is such a basic service in the West; we take it for granted. And yet it holds the key to global peace and prosperity.

To do the right thing, once we know what the right thing is, takes gumption. It is first determining what the right thing is that is the most difficult part.

18. Perspective in 'rock and a hard place' moments

When I worked as a summer camp counsellor in Canada, we used to play the 'bomb shelter' game with campers on overnight canoe trips.

Each of the campers was given a role to play – such as an 80-year-old engineer, a female Anglican priest, a hairdresser, a blind farmer, or a one-legged veterinarian. We had to pretend we were trapped in a bomb shelter after a thermonuclear war and confined to the shelter for at least 20 years until the radiation levels were safe enough to re-emerge. The only challenge was that there were not enough supplies to support everyone for the full 20 years. If some were to survive at all, at least three people had to leave the shelter. Who would be sent out to their death so the others could survive?

Vigorous debate ensued. Each person advocated the value of their role towards the future and current society. The point of the game for the campers was to raise the discussion of who and what we value as a society. It is also a classic ethical dilemma: is it OK to kill some so others may survive? This is a rock and hard place, as most of us feel that no deliberate death is a good result. In broad terms, we value life and each other.

While it's a hard debate, these discussions are easier in philosophical discussions than in real life.

On 7 January 2015, Corrine Rey, a cartoonist known as 'Coco' at the French satirical magazine *Charlie Hebdo*, returned to the office after picking up her daughter from kindergarten. She was confronted by two heavily armed men wearing balaclavas. They threatened to shoot her and her daughter unless she keyed in the entry code at the door to the office. She did, the gunmen rushed in, and Miss Rey and her daughter hid under a desk where they saw two other cartoonists being shot. The gunmen murdered 12 people in all (including two policemen), as well as shooting and injuring 11 others.

How would you feel if you let armed gunmen in to your workplace and saw them kill your colleagues? Should Corrine Rey have been willing to sacrifice her daughter and herself rather than allow masked, armed men to enter the magazine office and possibly kill everyone? Can a mother be blamed for only thinking of protecting her child?

Ethical dilemmas like these are rife in literature and movies.

In the 1982 movie *Sophie's Choice*, starring Meryl Streep and Kevin Kline, a Polish woman, Sophie Zawistowska, is arrested by the Nazis and sent to the Auschwitz concentration camp. On arrival, she is given a choice: one of her children will be spared the gas chamber. And she gets to choose – will it be her son or her daughter? She has only one minute, and they are both being dragged away. Either one of them dies, or both of them die. Suddenly, she lets go of her daughter. She is younger and smaller, and maybe her older, stronger son will survive the camp. He gets dragged away too, fate unknown. How does a mother live with this choice? How do you decide who has the better right to life?

As leaders in the corporate world, we are not often faced with life or death decisions, but we do confront significant ethical dilemmas. In a downsize, who do we make redundant – the alcoholic father with a severely disabled child who needs round-the-clock care? Or the Syrian refugee who hopes to bring her family out of Syria, who suffers from post-traumatic stress, and who has occasional loud, violent outbursts? Both are competent in their work, both have behavioural issues that impact others, and both have dependents in difficult circumstances.

What should you do?

From Aristotle onwards, much has been written on ethics. We have long asked the question: "What is the right thing to do?" Laws and religious rules created guidance on doing the right thing. In spite of all this, there are times when our moral compass spins wildly as choices challenge us to choose between one value and another.

19. Making decisions with the Meaning – Magnitude – Measure framework

With an ethical framework we can work out the best (or least worst) choices to make. Here is the framework I developed to help put decisions through various filters. By going through them, we put decisions through a rinse cycle, and wash out as much dirt as possible.

Before considering the framework, the first step to take is not on this chart, and is simply known as the "Sunlight Test". The question is: "Would I be happy with this on the front page of the newspaper (or trending on Twitter)?" This first question often cleans up a lot of poor behaviours. This could apply to both pressing pause on a reactive email or making the hard choices in an ethical dilemma.

	SELF	OTHERS	ORGANISATION/COMMUNITY
MEANING	What are the consequences for me?	What are the consequences for others?	What are the consequences for the organisation and community?
MAGNITUDE	What would happen if I did this all the time?	What would happen if others did this?	What would happen if organisations operated by this?
MEASURE	Is this consistent with my values?	What is the benefit versus harm?	Is this in line with Universal Principles?

Figure 3: The Meaning – Magnitude – Measure framework

After that, we can put your decision through three filters of meaning, magnitude, and measure, each with widening spheres of concern from self through to organisation, community, and ultimately the planet and universal concerns.

Meaning: Next look at the consequences of your decision for self, other, organisation, and the broader community.

Magnitude: Then explore the ripple effect of your decision. What is the effect on me and my character if I chose this consistently? What would happen if everyone acted like this? What if an organisation, community, or nation acted like this?

Measure: This is where you benchmark your decision against guidelines of good behaviour. The first sphere of concern is against our own personal values. Is this decision consistent with our values and beliefs? Next we look at the balance of harm versus benefit – is this a good outcome? And lastly, is this in line with larger Universal Principles?

Universal Principles are more difficult to agree on. However there are two that speak to our fundamental humanity:

1. **The Golden Rule:** Do to others as you would have them do to you. This rule is expressed consistently in all major religions.

2. **The fundamental value of every human being.** The Universal Declaration of Human Rights, developed by the UN General Assembly, asserts this as a global principle on which we can build a world of peace, justice, and freedom.

Going through these filters and putting choices through the rinse cycle won't guarantee everyone will agree with our decision. Moral disagreements are common. It may not be that universal agreement is the goal, but to know we did our best and put the decision to the test across several filters. The way we make decisions is the important thing. To know we made the hard choices in a way that is sincere and focused on doing right for self, others, and planet.

Ethical filters are a key to developing perspective that builds both conviction and courage in our choices.

Testing the Meaning – Magnitude – Measure framework

Let's test the framework in a scenario. My friend comes to me and tells me she is having an affair with her neighbour. She has been married for 20 years. She loves her husband, but is not in love with him anymore, and has found solace and adventure with her neighbour. She does not want to leave her husband. She wants to continue both relationships. She says, "I'm happier, so what is the harm? I'm actually nicer to my husband."

First off, I have a huge reaction. I feel a surge of judgement against my friend. It turns out loyalty is also one of my top values, as well as integrity, and here my friend is demonstrating neither. Not loyalty to her husband, nor integrity in wanting to perpetuate a betrayal of vows. I feel a bristle of negativity.

What should I do? Tell the husband? He is also my friend. Is it my place to intervene in a marriage? What if someone else tells him first and he found out I knew and said nothing? What about my friend who confided in me? Do I break her confidence? Is any of this my business?

This is hard. I'm leaning towards not saying anything.

It's possible however that short-term pain will lead to long-term happiness. I have seen this many times as couples split and ultimately become happier because they are living authentic lives.

Avoiding causing pain is at the heart of why people don't speak up. We make excuses for the abusive spouse because we fear that splitting the family is worse. We make excuses for our alcoholic colleague who shows up late for work because we don't want her to lose her job. We secretly hope that she will sort herself out – go to a support group, resolve her personal issues, and stop drinking. That would be the best scenario, for her to take responsibility for herself and her life. But she doesn't, and we dance around it, avoiding pulling the trigger that will cause a cascade of painful short-term consequences. "Not my business" we tell ourselves. "It's her life", we say. "She's a grown up, she can look after herself. Who am I to pass judgement on her?"

Let's put the decision of my staying silent about my neighbour through the ethics-rinsing framework.

Sunlight test first: Here is the tweet: "Woman betrays trust of best friend (BF) and tells husband of BF that BF has been cheating on him."

I'm ok with that.

Meaning: What are the consequences for me, for them and the family, for the community? For me, it's knowing I betrayed my friend's confidence and brought pain to my other friend. For them, it means confronting a dishonesty. Their marriage may or may not survive. And there are kids involved. What's best for them? Not sure.

Magnitude: What would happen if I made the choice to stay silent all the time? This feels like I might end up being the person who says, "It's none of my business". What if everyone behaved in this way? Would we have groupthink? Blind obedience? Chronic complacency?

Measure: Is the decision to stay silent consistent with my values? Actually, no. Honesty and integrity are my core values. What is the balance of benefit versus harm? I can't see much benefit to staying silent, except that ignorance is bliss. I suspect there will be a lot of pain – mostly from my guilty conscience and feeling complicit in the deception. Is the decision of silence in line with Universal Principles? I think if my partner was cheating, I would want my friend to tell me, no matter how hard it would be for them. Why? Because not telling denies the second Universal Principle of the universal value of every human being. Denial is not respectful.

So, as I rinse the decision through the ethical framework, I realise that staying silent is not how I will proceed. I would first encourage my friend to be honest herself first. I would let her know that the choice to be in a three-party relationship should also include her husband's decision on that point.

I think if I had to deliver this news it would be a very painful experience, and I'm not sure now that it would feel very good at the end. But having gone through the exercise I think I could feel good about my convictions and the process I went through to address the dilemma.

What about you?

20. Speaking up and challenging convention

Scenario 1: Making a stand against 'standards'

Charlotte is a quiet and sensitive girl of nine. She attends a small private primary school in a coastal Australian town. It's winter, and the uniform is a thick wool dress, stiff buttoned long sleeve top, and woolly tights. It looks smart.

But it's damn uncomfortable. Charlotte is frustrated with the dress. She can't kick the soccer ball properly and she certainly can't climb on the monkey bars, as the dress will lift up and expose her panties. She watches the boys enviously as they scamper around the playground. She wants to run and play like them.

Charlotte goes home and asks her mother, "Mum can I wear my sport uniform tomorrow?" This is a big no-no. You are only allowed to wear sports uniform on sports day. Tomorrow is not a sports day. Her mother pauses and looks at her, "Why do you want to do that, Charlotte?"

"Because the winter dress is uncomfortable." Her mother presses her a little, sensing there is more to the story. "I can't play soccer and I can't go on the monkey bars properly." She looks embarrassed to say in front of her Dad, "When I hang upside-down on the monkey bars it shows my underpants."

Her mum Josie concedes. "OK – go ahead, you can wear your sports uniform."

The next day Josie gets a call from the school. Why was Charlotte not in proper uniform? Josie explains what Charlotte had said, about it being uncomfortable and restrictive. The school official seems ruffled.

A day later, Josie gets a letter addressed to 'All Parents'. It states that children are to dress in the winter uniform, wear proper shoes, and tidy up their appearance. Josie notes this part: "There are standards to uphold."

School officials do not give a satisfactory response to her further questions, saying there are only ten days left of winter term anyway. In the meantime, Charlotte continues to wear her sports uniform to school. The other children tease her and ask her why. She flushes red, and says, "Because it's not right. It's not fair that the boys can wear pants and play outside and we can't because of the dress."

For nine-year-old Charlotte, this is as much a question of comfort as it was a question of equality. Why are the girls required to wear constrictive dresses that hamper their ability to fully participate and learn – *like the boys*? It was clear sexism. And the only answer from the school is that it was about 'standards'.

An awkward compromise is reached. Charlotte can wear her sports uniform, as long as she wears the dress on days where there are official functions, like speech and awards days. She agrees.

This protest is momentous. A nine-year-old took on the school system under enormous pressure from adults in positions of authority, and the ridicule of her peers. This kind of social pressure is enormous at any age, let alone nine!

Scenario 2: Speaking out against overwork

Toni Hoffman knew something was not quite right. She was Head Nurse at the Intensive Care Unit at Bundaberg Hospital. She had noticed just too many patients with serious complications. All of them came after the surgery performed by Jayant Patel. She raised her concerns with hospital management and other staff, but nothing happened. The Queensland Health District Manager and the hospital's Director of Medical Services largely ignored more than 20 complaints regarding Patel. Why?

At Bundaberg Hospital, there was a culture of celebrating overwork. Patel worked extremely long hours and performed a huge number of procedures. This was seen as a boon to the hospital. At one stage he was even made employee of the month. Hoffman experienced ridicule and derision from her peers for challenging his work and raising these concerns. The issues with recovering patients continued. Frustrated by the lack of response from the hospital, Hoffman decided to go public, and spoke to her local MP, Rob Messenger. There was an inquiry.

On 1 July 2010, five years after the issues surfaced from 2003-2005, Patel was sentenced to seven years' jail. He was found guilty of three charges of manslaughter, and one count of grievous bodily harm. It was not until May 2015 that Patel was finally disbarred from practicing medicine in Australia.

In 2006, Toni Hoffman received the Order of Australia medal and the Local Hero Award. She took legal action against Queensland Health for gross negligence in failing to care for her through her whistleblowing activities, and for denying her requests for specialised counselling. She received compensation in a private settlement.

Speaking up for the greater good takes courage and conviction. There is real risk of social derision, professional suicide, and ongoing health challenges.

Scenario 3: Challenging the experts

My Dad was seriously uncomfortable. It was two days after his bowel cancer surgery and he was meant to be heading home. A British gentleman from the early Baby Boomer generation, Dad had been well-schooled in keeping a tight upper lip, remaining stoic, and not complaining.

He politely mentioned to the doctor that he felt like there was a blockage in his abdomen.

The doctor reassured him it was just the natural pains of recovering from surgery.

When Dad started vomiting like a firehose around the room, they started to take more notice. They checked his blood pressure, and his breathing and pulse was rapid. This was not the usual recovery pattern. They tried feeding him jelly. Rancid red spray ensued. They tried sips of water. Dry retching followed. His belly swelled, and he looked poorly.

The doctors harrumphed.

One of the young interns who was doing her practical experience on the ward took Dad's vitals. His breathing was laboured, his belly was uncomfortable. The intern suggested they should take a chest X-ray and see if there was something unusual happening. They wheeled Dad into X-ray. The films came back and the eyebrows went up. Where there was meant to be plenty of dark space was now nearly filled. Dad was filling up with fluids from his bowels. The re-section had fallen apart, and his bowels were emptying shit into his abdominal cavity.

Thirty minutes later Dad was in an induced coma, fighting for his life as the emergency medical staff tried to drain his abdomen of the septic mess that was quickly poisoning him. It was an in intern who spoke up and saved my Dad's life.

This was a real act of heroic courage.

I find most doctors are pretty assertive in their opinions. They seem to have a natural arrogance that comes from years of in-depth immersion into expertise. The more specialised the expertise, the more exaggerated the hubris.

If we question an expert's opinion or approach, we often receive a very defensive and dismissive response. When I asked my cancer specialist what I could do to help my healing along (being interested in mind-body connection and the power of the body to heal itself through positive thought, meditation and nutrition), my doctor – the leading gynaecological oncologist in Australia – responded flatly, "There is nothing you can do to change the tumour. It needs to be cut out."

And so I believed him. After all, who I am to question a man who has years of both study and experience?

We defer to expertise. We defer to authority. We defer to uniforms.

— ◻ —

Robert Cialdini wrote a seminal book called *Influence: The psychology of persuasion* (2006).[27] In this book he describes how one of the key defaults we have as humans is the respect for authority. It is hard-wired into our social psyche to trust and obey the people in charge. After all, they are meant to be looking out for us. We will do all sorts of heinous behaviour if someone with a uniform, a title, or even dressed well asks us or tells us. This helps maintain social order and harmony, and helps ensure our survival as a group. Follow the leader; they are looking out for us.

What happens if the leader is wrong?

We don't like to think they could be wrong. If they're wrong, if our protectors, our elders, are wrong, then how can we ever feel safe? What are we to trust in, if not the experience and expertise of our elders?

To question our leaders and question authority is to invite fear into the tribe. And nothing creates a more primal response than uncertainty. Once that amygdala gets activated, we shut down our capacity for rational thought and we are in survival mode.

To question the leader is to trigger unease. It's not comfortable. It threatens our world order.

When that lovely young intern suggested an X-ray, she was questioning her leader, a man of 30 years of specialised medical training and experience in one of the USA's most prestigious and well-respected hospitals.

Why would anyone listen to an intern over the doctor? She had no credibility and no experience. This was her first bowel cancer re-section, and she knew enough from her recent studies to see that laboured breathing was an abdominal area issue. She had not tried to join the dots of previous surgeries, simply because she had no previous experience.

So she rocked the boat and suggested that since it seemed to be a chest issue, maybe they should do a chest X-ray.

To his credit, the doctor agreed. And my Dad survived. Just. He was very close to multiple organ failure and had nine days in a coma, four wash out procedures, and then two months of intensive rehabilitation.

Why speaking up is hard

There are three things at risk for a leader in speaking up:

1. **Belongingness:** We fear criticising our peers and leaders. This seems disloyal.

2. **Social exclusion:** We fear anger and retribution from others. We are threatening the safety of the tribe.

3. **Being the pariah:** We fear being labelled a tattle-tale, a robber, an informant. These are accusations of being personally motivated rather than focused on altruistic motives.

Belongingness triggers a deep primal response. Brené Brown says: "We are spiritually, emotionally, physically wired to belong. And when we don't, we ache, we hurt, we break, we fall apart, we hurt others…"[28]

Integral Leadership Development Stages

Our primary stage of leadership development may also affect our resolve to speak up. There is an integrated leadership development model for adult stages of learning and growth focuses on 'action logic' – how we perceive and engage with each other and the world.[29]

Our action logic responds to shifting contexts. The main premises of developmental stages are:

1. Adults may continue to develop their thinking and worldview once they become adults. Development does not cease at official legal age.

2. Context can cause human thinking and action to evolve in response to new dynamics, interests, responsibilities, and pressures.

3. How we see the world and our place in it shapes how we engage with others, how we make decisions, what we focus on, and what kind of results we experience in our work and lives.

4. A leader and their social group have different concerns and actions in a tribal agrarian survival scenario than a leader in a corporate multinational office focused on solving non-fossil fuel energy solutions. The thinking, interacting and expectations of each leader will be completely different due to their context. Their thinking evolves, in part, as a result of their surroundings.

Bill Torbert and others contend that individuals evolve their leadership thinking through common patterns:

· The individualistic survival perspective of the **opportunist**

· The social security and bonds of following the status quo of the **diplomat**

· The rise of independent thinking through experience and learning leads to the **expert** mindset

· The collective focus of the **achiever** who knows that a team delivers better results than the lone wolf

· The obsessive interest in multiple truths and perspectives of the **individualist**

· The **strategist** who holds organisational and social transformation as their core focus.

Interestingly, less evolved worldviews can exist in technologically advanced societies.

In the opportunist outlook, there is not much leadership going on, unless it is gang-related. This is when there has been a marginal shift in leadership perspective, where the lone criminal has worked out that he or she might be more effective in a cohort of criminals. There is a leadership of sorts, but it's one of power and brute strength rather than collaboration and inspiration. If leadership choices are happening, it is driven by one-upmanship – our tribe against the rest of the world. There is no sense of the collective.

In our development, one of the first big shifts – from renegade lone wolf opportunist to the collective safety of the tribe in the diplomat stage – marks the deep connection we have to tribe, to community, and sense of safety,

If we raise an issue that threatens the safety of the tribe, it is akin to brandishing a sword in the King's hall. The leader is threatened, the sanctity of the safe sacred space is injured and insulted, and the whole tribe goes on alert. In raising an issue that rattles the foundations or reputation of the organisation, we have gone from concerned tribe member to ostracised traitor.

Why your voice matters

One in seven people on the planet log on to Facebook every day. That's 1.43 billion people. The opportunity for global connection and interaction is mind-boggling! And the potential for amplifying messages is boundless and immediate. This goes for messages of peace and love as much as it does for messages of hate and vilification.

The sad truth is that most of us don't bother to speak up when we see something that we think and feel is wrong. We have all sorts of reasons not to:

- Don't want to rock the boat
- Don't want to lose my job
- Don't want to get involved
- It's not my business anyway.

We keep squarely to the little patch carved around us. We stick our head in the sand and pretend it will all be OK. Except that it's not and it won't be. This is how tyrants rise. These excuses above are actually symptoms of more insidious hidden problems:

- Unchallenged loyalty
- Blind deference to authority
- Playing victim to avoid responsibility.

We are hardwired for loyalty and obedience. This has ensured the success of our species: band together to avoid threat from the 'other'. When we obey and defer to our tribal leader, we keep the tribe strong. This is why whistleblowers are so maligned: when they call their leaders or their tribe's way of doing things to account, other tribe members feel their safety is compromised. From the tribe's point of view, it's better to destroy the usurper and protect the status quo.

Challenge to authority threatens the integrity and thus the safety of the tribe. In *Influence: The psychology of persuasion* (1984), Robert Cialdini describes some frightening experiments where people will do the most extraordinary, horrible things to others if asked by people in apparent authority roles. It explains how otherwise normal, caring people turned into Nazis.

But most of us are not sheltering in caves with one eye out for hungry predators and the other for threatening neighbours. We are global citizens with interconnected economies. We need each other.

Speaking up requires that we overcome our own biological urges for connection and safety of the tribe. It means we'll be seen. If speaking up means we need to fight the fear of being attacked, or of being excluded from the tribe, why on earth should we bother?

Here are some compelling reasons:

- We avoid complacency in the face of injustice
- We stop being complicit in the face of inequity
- We add colour and depth to conversation, avoiding the grey-beige of status quo
- We stop playing victim and take charge of our own life.

And yet I know this is sometimes not enough to strum the courage chords within.

When we don't speak up, we sail close to shore in the 'safe' shallows of unfulfilled potential. Our ship of life is a grand vessel. It is not meant to keep to shore. In the shallows it gathers barnacles, and the keel tangles in weeds. If we look out to sea, just past the headland where the water turns a little rough and wild, we see the drowning face of our captain: the person of integrity we always thought we could have been.

It's never too late. We can learn to speak up, and steer our ship out to sea, and save the captain of our soul.

This is the choice that Charlotte made at school. It is the same choice Toni Hoffman made at work. It is the same choice the young intern made with her boss. Speaking up was a personal risk for each person. The personal risk was weighed up against principle, and in the latter two cases, against the lives of others. In this way, speaking up is a deeply personal self-reinforcing act, and at the same time profoundly purposeful and selfless. These two reasons together help trump any self-protective mechanisms that would keep our voices quiet.

21. Why be a truth-teller?

How confident are you in the future? Do you have a great sense of certainty about how the world will be in five years? In ten? Organisations that stick doggedly to their five-year strategy with fierce commitment are likely to die too. How many bookstores, CD stores, DVD hire places do you see around these days? This is failure to adapt.

These organisations were likely missing a **truth-teller.**

A truth-teller is a person who speaks the truth, especially when the truth is not a popular perspective. A truth-teller shines a light on uncomfortable facts. They may call attention to a project that is failing, or a social dynamic that is dysfunctional, or a trend that is threatening to wipe demand for a product aside.

Truth-tellers have also been called 'soothsayers', or 'seers.' These people have existed in most cultures around the globe. A soothsayer was a person who spoke truth, often practising divination, fortune-telling, oracles, or haruspicy (the lovely art of inspecting entrails for signs of future events). Through history, soothsayers have always had troubled experiences. If they tell a story that resonates and uplifts, they are celebrated. When they bring bad tidings, they are maligned, ostracised, and sometimes killed.

Being a contemporary truth-teller is akin to the treacherous life of a soothsayer. Speaking the truth does not always bring good news, and can be confronting for people. A modern-day truth-teller might reveal:

· *The business plan is flawed and will likely spin the organisation into disaster.*

   The team will react defensively, as it was their plan;
   the comment is seen as a personal criticism.

· *The team is run by a forceful leader who imposes their will on others.*

   No-one contradicts the boss out of fear of reprisal and losing favour.

· *A project is doomed, as there is simply no longer demand in the market.*

   Team members fight for the project because the alternative means contending with potential job loss and failure.

· *Internal politics are corroding collaboration and team morale, and results are failing.*

Factions bind together in self-defence. The best form of defence is attack, especially against the truth-teller.

· *Some roles in the organisation are superfluous and draining the business of financial resources.*

No-one likes being told they are a waste of space or under-performing; insult turns to attack.

Self-protection against a truth-teller's observations creates huge blind spots for an organisation. The fierce drive for personal survival supersedes the need to rise above the truth and bind together in exploring new options. Instead we often default to fighting for the status quo.

What we need is three-fold:

1. **We need to encourage and celebrate the truth-tellers.** They say what we dare not admit. They reveal what we most fear. And in doing so, we are freed from the shackles of being timid. They invite us to dare, to pioneer, to explore, to risk, and in doing so, they give us the best chance of surviving.

2. **We need to become a truth-teller ourselves.** We need to hone our skills of looking at the current and future trends and understand what they mean, good and bad. We need to become brave in asking the tough questions, to point out the elephants lounging in the middle of the room. We need to get curious about what we are seeing. If the Emperor has no clothes, then we say so.

3. **We need to speak the truth, without lobbing poo bombs.** Bad news is still bad news. If we develop rapport with others, if we hold a good intention, if we invite them with respect to discuss the troubling truth, then we have a better chance of not setting off a poo bomb and its subsequent poo-storm. We can learn to speak the truth, ease the pain, and keep the players at the table. This is masterful truth-telling.

22. How to make a courageous choice

All the moments that matter are a test of our personal power. Do we or don't we? Do we say it or not say it? Do we stand up or hide out? Do we speak up or shut down? Ultimately, how we choose, not what we choose, defines our essence as a leader. The impact we have or don't have all boils down to that nanosecond of choice: What do I do?

Personal power is the energy that drives us forward or holds us back. The capacity to make decisions in ambiguous circumstances, in black and white situations, where the choices seem to sandwich us between a rock and hard place, is our single most important leadership resource.

Personal power is built first as your character castle. This is the essence of who you are as a person, and the daily habits that sustain you. Having a framework to make difficult decisions gives you the how for your courageous choices. Keeping a moat around your character castle is also critical – this is all about maintaining strong personal boundaries.

How to develop personal power

Build your Character Castle, the baseline of personal power

Personal power needs strong foundations. This is the essence of your core identity as a person and as a leader. It's an holistic reinforcement of your best attributes that will sustain in you in difficult times. From here your character can be built as strong and big as a castle.

1. **Construct** a solid personal identity and a useful definition of success. I covered this in great detail in *Composure*.

2. **Craft** a strong physicality with self-care and self-talk. Again, a core principle of *Composure*.

3. **Collect** compliments, results, and evidence of your awesomeness. Trust me, you will need this! Leaders have bad days, and when you have one, you will need some evidence and reminders that you are not scum of the earth (as your detractors might

allege), but that you are in fact a decent human being, with a long list of achievements and feel-good moments. I keep a success diary to track my achievements and efforts. I keep folder of feedback, cards, and compliments in a file I call 'Nice Things For Me'.

These three basic skills build courage, conviction, and confidence. And yet we can often self-sabotage with our own internal voice.

The sticks we whack ourselves with

Deflection, denigration, and dissolution

When I meet a new client for private leadership mentoring, the conversation sometimes goes like this: "I struggle with my colleagues. Relationships are not my best skill. I'm overworked and find it hard to say no and cope with what is asked of me. My work is slipping, things are tense at home, and I'm feeling swamped."

It's a pattern I often see: a poor inner narrative expressed as leadership challenges. We let our inner poop sabotage our capacity for connection and influence. This devilish triad is:

· Deflection

· Denigration

· Dissolution.

I wince every time I hear expressions of these. It's like watching someone whack themselves with a barbed stick. We have a disease of self-flagellation and it's shackling our ability to be who we need to be in moments that matter most. With our family, with our colleagues, with our clients.

Deflection

Deflection is the martial art of inner demons. It's when we deflect all good things that come to us: compliments, reassurance, hugs, help, assistance. We have an enormous shield that we wield, watching for incoming expressions of appreciation and admiration.

Why?

We may have a default inner narrative that goes something like, "I'm not good enough, I'm not worthy, they don't really mean it, they're just being nice." Where does this come from? Likely from some deep recess of our childhood days. It doesn't matter. We don't want to wallow in it and breathe more life into this unhelpful inner recording. It's akin to wailing and crying to the skies, "mea culpa, mea culpa!" This is a salve to the inner demons.

We must replace that inner demon with something more constructive.

Denigration

Denigration is the battering rod of the inner demons. It's how we punish ourselves for being inadequate and disappointing. We know the inner demons are in full swing when we catch ourselves saying, "I'm such an idiot! I can't believe I did that! I really suck at that. I screwed up. I'm such a loser."

Denigration occurs every time we finish the phrase, "I am..." with something negative, or if we criticise our efforts without any learning or application. Sometimes we do screw up. We make mistakes. We react rather than respond. We overlook something important. This is only a problem if:

· It's a chronic pattern

· We don't learn from it

· We didn't really try.

I have yet to meet a leader who doesn't really try. The ones with the worst demons are those who try the most! So why the inner demon of denigration?

We haven't learned to turn our inner critic to an inner critique. Again, it's likely a pattern that emerged from some dark and damaging incident or experience from our more impressionable days that we haven't fully healed from.

It doesn't matter where it came from. We can change it.

Dissolution

Dissolution is probably the worst of the devilish weapons. It is a crushing of self for an alleged noble cause. Cue all the martyrs here.

This looks like the mother who works all day, rushes home to make dinner, does laundry, tidies the house, and feeds herself last. It is sometimes known as the 'burnt chop' syndrome. If at a barbecue, the mother will feed all the good meat to her partner, the children, and the guests, and then nibble what is left – usually the burnt chop.

In men, it's the 'good father' syndrome: bust your butt all day at work, poignantly aware that you're responsible for feeding many mouths, rush home to take over parenting duties, play with kids, chauffeur them around to sport activities, and on the weekend do errands, fix things around the house (because that is what manly men do), and maybe sneak a beer in there somewhere. These men are often on antidepressants.

It's the self-last principle at play. It's based on good intentions: to be a good parent; be a good boss; be a good friend.

Now I've deliberately exaggerated stereotypes to make a point. And it's not just leaders with families. There are plenty of leaders who do everyone else's bidding – for friends, for family, for their colleagues and supervisor, and leave themselves last. The truth is that martyrs end up dead. Metaphorically, our true self ends up dead. We dissolve our identity, our soul, in service to other people.

Why?

Because that's what we're supposed to do: be good to other people. It's a poor rationale for self-effacement. Deflection and denigration are deep expressions of denial of our own worthiness. The triad of devilishness is really a recipe for self-destruction. If we don't master this, we let our own personal mess poop all over our personal power.

If we don't master the devilish triad of deflection, denigration, and dissolution, we have no hope of making the most of moments that matter, let alone recognising them.

— ¤ —

Finding bravery on the cliff's edge: A framework for difficult choices

One of my favourite activities on outdoor experiential programs is abseiling (rappelling for my North American buddies). It's a pretty unnatural task: walk backwards over a cliff edge, only attached by some metal parts and a rope. People generally feel anxious about it. This is probably a good thing. If you didn't have natural apprehension around gigantic drops where you might plunge to your death, you probably don't have great risk management.

In my experience in the outdoors, I've discovered an important distinction when it comes to bravery. It's actually not found on the edge of the cliff.

The moment of truth comes well before that. It comes in the decision-making on the ground, before stepping up for your turn. An abseiling briefing may take 30 minutes as all the processes are explained and demonstrated. In that time, the individual is considering the options: do I do it, or not?

By the time they step up to get clipped in, they have already decided. Then they simply follow through, step by step, backwards over a cliff. I'm not saying that all the anxiety is resolved! Having committed to the process, they work their way through it. Very few turn back at the top once they are roped in.

Most people flop their way through a courageous decision. They feel nervous, they fret, they watch others go first, they rehearse worst-case scenarios in their head, they worry about how others will see them, and then talk themselves in to taking action.

Difficult decisions that require courage get easier when we have developed the capacity to make them. Like a knight training for an epic quest, we can practice the fundamentals that prepare for us battle with dragons, trolls, and assorted demons. These are Define, Decide, and Deliver.

Define your choice by what it says about you as a person.

- What does this choice say about who I am? Am I happy with that?

- What identity do I project with this choice? Am I comfortable with that?

- What values do I demonstrate with this choice? Does this choice align with my core values? Am I acting with integrity?

- How does this support my beliefs?

Decide on a course of action (doing nothing is also a choice).

- Given the knowledge and options at the time, is this the best option for most concerned?
- Am I prepared to accept the consequences?
- Procrastination is also a decision. What am I deciding by not doing anything? What does this say about me, my character, and my values?

Deliver is actually taking action.

- Am I half-hearted or all in?
- What does failure mean to me?
- How do I define success?
- How will I manage shame?
- How will I manage guilt?
- How can I process my fear and apprehension so they fuel me and do not paralyse me?

Most people don't filter their decisions on the precipice this way. They are buffeted by the winds of their internal dialogue, directed largely by the amygdala, the survival mechanism. Rational thought gets shut down and the protection instinct kicks in.

With practice, Define, Decide, and Deliver becomes less clunky, and more fluid.

The conscious and self-aware leader learns to process their thinking and focus deliberately. They reach for what matters most, and this drives a decision. It gives momentum to act with courage. By the time they step up to the cliff's edge, they are resolute. They may be afraid, but they are committed. The leader's decision is one that reinforces who they are and what they want. They will allow the power of alignment to keep them from fear. Then it's one step at time, over the edge.

How do you go on the precipice? What moves you to step over or back away? How do you build courage? What keeps you from

taking one step at a time?

23. Boundaries

How to develop a 'boundaries moat' around your castle

In trying to be accommodating and helpful, sometimes we make choices that are not in our best interest, and more to please others. We end up sacrificing our free time, our energy, and sometimes even our money – all in the interest of being helpful. If we do this too much and too often, we can start to feel uncomfortable at first, perhaps a bit downtrodden and taken advantage of, and then resentful.

The key work here is to develop strong boundaries, or rules of engagement. This is what is OK and not OK in a relationship, personal or professional. When expressing our boundaries, we need to be clear about why the boundary is important to us, identify the behaviour that is not comfortable, and ask the other person to behave differently.

Here is an example:

> "Simon, when you email me at 2am and expect an answer immediately I feel this is having a negative impact on me. It is disrupting my sleep, increasing my anxiety levels, and frustrating my partner who is also getting woken up. What I'd prefer instead is that all non-life threatening messages be kept to business hours."

This is not as crazy as an example as you would think! There are workplaces where boundaries have eroded so dramatically that being interrupted in the middle of the night on something urgent (but not at all life threatening) has become common practice.

When we put boundaries in place, this can feel like challenging the status quo, especially if the workplace culture has come to accept this kind of behaviour as the norm. This is why doing boundaries work can be so challenging!

Insight

In our personal relationships, boundaries are easily eroded. My very first experience with this was with a boyfriend, George. I had many assumptions about what a healthy, respectful relationship should look like. It was obvious to me: equal partners, equal participation in the relationship. Equal participation meant equal finances, equal chores in housekeeping, and equal respect.

Things weren't equal, however. I was his boss for one. I earned more money than him for another. It was my apartment for a third. I was older than him for a fourth. I owned a car, he didn't. I believed in a healthy lifestyle and was training for a marathon. He was overweight and smoked pot. I hate pot. Plus, he did it at work. And that put me in an awkward position. He forced me into a double-standard: reprimanding and disciplining others who smoked cigarettes and pot, while he did the same. He made me look like a hypocrite.

My internal dialogue went like this:

"Doesn't he know he is putting me in an unprofessional double bind? I can't act with integrity on this issue. I feel forced into choosing my career over the relationship – based on pot, of all the stupid things to risk a career on! Plus, he never pays for petrol. I always pay for petrol. But he always takes the car – my car – and drives it everywhere. He doesn't offer to pay for the insurance, the upkeep or the petrol. He doesn't pay for groceries either."

I felt completely used and disrespected. What an asshole!

In fact, I was being the asshole. For all George knew, I was perfectly happy with the arrangements. I just seethed through clenched teeth.

After I learned about the value of boundaries from my very first Executive Coach Gary Russell, I gathered my courage skirts about me. One night, while cooking dinner (with groceries I bought), I blurted out, "I think you should pay for half the petrol." My face burned, my heart thumped.

He looked at me, surprised, and said, "Sure."

That was it.

After the build-up in my mind about this issue, I was a little disappointed. I was expecting push back, resistance, criticism. Something. Not agreement. Not so easily! So I blundered my way through an explanation of how I felt like I was being taken advantage of, and how it was better if we shared this expense.

He said, "OK."

Wow. That was it. Agreement on my first boundary issue! I felt elated! What a triumph! This stuff actually works! All the money I was spending on the Executive Coach was totally worth it for the feeling of victory I had in that moment.

A week later, George indicated he was willing to pitch in for petrol, without any prompting from me. I was now ready to tackle the pot issue.

I had my opening remarks prepared. "George, when you smoke pot around the work premises I feel really uncomfortable. As a senior staff member it's my duty to report any illegal activities, and our personal relationship puts me in a compromising position. What I would prefer is that you stopped smoking pot."

Phew. Message delivered using the perfect feedback formula, "when you...I feel...I prefer... "

He said, "Well it's illegal to plant weeds in the river corridor."

"Ummm.... What?"

"It's illegal to plant weeds in the river corridor. The strawberries, gardenias you planted, are all weeds. Your garden is illegal."

What?

I tried again. "You're compromising my position…"

"You're doing illegal stuff."

Seriously, what the hell?

I tried again. Same response. I was getting seriously pissed off by this point. He was not hearing me at all. And there was in no way equivalent illegality of a garden and freakin' smoking pot! It did not end well. He got agitated, my face turned to purple with boiling rage, and for the first and only time in my life, I grabbed something and broke it. It turns out it was a Smurf figurine – his favourite toy from childhood.

Boundary not understood or respected. That relationship soon ended.

We assume people know what is the 'right' thing to do to treat us well. We assume we have the same levels or standards of behaviour, and are shocked when others have different standards. We take it as personal insults. It's not everybody else's job to read our minds!

People will either accept the boundary, or test it like a two-year-old, or argue about it. If they argue about it, as George did, then it's time to walk away. I chose integrity over a relationship.

24. What is true grit?

Grit is perseverance: the bloody-minded focus to keep going. The world shrinks to the next simple choice, and bit-by-bit, we get to somewhere else. The capacity for grit has to be honed. Sometimes we are thrown into a situation where we have no option but to grind away though adversity. In this trial by fire, we may discover inner resilience out of necessity.

Crawling out from under the canoe in the Canadian wilderness ignited a flame within me. If I could wrestle that beast from a difficult spot, what else could I do? How strong was I really? I embraced as many opportunities as I could to test myself and to see how far I could go.

I worked at summer camp for nine summers, paddling many more miles. I jumped at the chance to move around the world, not knowing a soul, to work for Outward Bound Australia. I learned to abseil, to raft, to bushwalk through rugged Aussie terrain and in scorching, dry heat. I learned cross-country skiing and went mountaineering in New Zealand. I put my hand up for senior roles at Outward Bound. I ran six marathons. I started my own business.

Every year I challenge myself to grow and learn and explore. I never knew I could do any of these things before I did them! And I was scared every time. But I still did them.

True grit over the coals

I once did an Anthony Robbins program called 'Unleash the Power Within', his iconic three-day workshop. It was in a huge auditorium filled with 5,000 people, the crowd was pumped up by dancers on stage and the best dance music throbbing all the way up to the rooftop struts. It was a full immersive experience – once I entered the doors, I was fully swamped with the pounding vibrations of optimism and excitement. I was dancing in my seat and smiling at strangers within two minutes. The days were long and there were rarely breaks. It seemed to go on and on in a vacuum of time.

The pinnacle of the first day was the famous firewalk. After storytelling from Tony (who is a giant of a man with a mesmerising style and endless energy), we were all jazzed up. Five thousand of us traipsed outside the stadium to the firewalking coals that had been prepared by the crew. There were dozens of these coal beds. I waited in line with the others, bopping and dancing to the still thudding music bonanza, doing my power moves to anchor my sense of strength and determination.

And then it was my turn. One of the staff grabbed me by the shoulders stared into my eyes, and asked in a strong assertive voice: "Are you ready?" "Yes!" I shouted. He asked me again, shouting this time, "Are you READY?" "YES!" I screamed back with delirious excitement.

"OK – go."

And off I pounced, chanting the refrain, "cool moss, cool moss", staring at the end of the coals with the waiting crew cheering me on. I stomped easily across the coals and was caught at the end, people whooping and hugging and slapping me on the back.

It was awesome.

So where is the firewalk when you need it most? Where is the firewalk when you have a board meeting and you know they are going to nail you on the sub-par performance of your project? Tony Robbins teaches the mastery of emotional states. He claims you can use the experience of the firewalk to bring back that sense of achievement and invincibility when it matters most.

25. How to develop true grit

Peak experiences and novel situations that test your mettle are an excellent way to reinforce confidence. It is the essence of my work in the outdoors: take people into new situations where their usual resources and familiarity are removed, and see how they can develop new patterns and discover new capabilities.

What I find with leaders, however, is that many of them have a mountain of exceptional experiences. They are huge achievers. They've cycled thousands of kilometres for charities, overcome debilitating illnesses, recovered from childhood abuses, stood in the firestorms of public criticism and survived.

Build your power from the inside-out

Looking at me, you would never guess that I have run marathons, done mountaineering, or hiked in remote areas. I am shaped like cuddly teddy bear rather than sleek athlete. However, I never let my biology dictate my ability. I have set about discovering what my body can do, regardless of the shape it is. That's the whole point of developing true grit. You don't what you are capable of until you try it.

That's the other point about true grit: it is built little by little, moment by moment.

Peak experiences like the firewalk remind us what we are capable of. The daily work of true grit is more banal, but is what builds the inner iron bar, that deep and powerful presence.

How to design a true grit project

Next you need to develop ongoing, regular, self-designed crucibles to keep your comfort zone flexible and not brittle. Think of something that scares you at least a little. The tingly tummy kind of scared. Not the white-knuckle kind. There are different types of true grit projects:

· **Physical ones:** Marathon, climb, run, swim, belly dance

- **Cognitive ones:** Write a book, learn a new skill, or language
- **Emotional ones:** Forgive, speak up, go dating.

With a new experience in mind, complete the sentence, "I could never ..." (Climb mountains / run marathons / speak in public / ask someone out on a date / write a book / learn Japanese cooking).

1. Ask yourself the following questions: "Do I want to? Why or why not?"

2. Then ask: "Will it help me to feel better / be more confident? Connect better with others? Discover new thresholds? Help others?"

3. Finally, ask yourself: "Do I have to re-define who I am through this crucible?"

Do all these pass the back-of-neck tingle / tummy butterfly test?

Once your true grit project is firmly in your line of sight, it's time to get real. Any true grit project needs structure, a measure of progress, and support. Here are some key tips:

Accountability: When you make your project public, even if it is only to one person, it is easier to honour this commitment. For my first marathon, I knew my sister was flying over to Australia from Montreal to run it with me. I had to be ready so I would not let her down.

Progress: This is critical. It's important to document how far you've come so you don't get demoralised by how far there is to go. By making progress visible, you can celebrate the small wins along the way to your big goal. When I was training for a marathon, I had my 12-week running plan in my journal, and I would tick off each workout day-by-day. This helped me feel prepared for the big run, even if I was nervous. Knowing I had done all the work I needed to gave me confidence. It also helped me feel proud of myself that I'd honoured my commitments and showed up each day for the training.

Support / mentor: Crucible experiences are tough. Having someone to guide or cheer you helps get you through. I remember my very first 21km run. It was the longest I had ever run, and I knew it would take me over two hours. Even though the weather forecast was for bucketing rain, I was committed to getting through it. About halfway through it, my friend and supervisor at the time, Sam Robinson, drove by. She slowed up beside me and said, "Wow! You're doing great! I think you're actually going to do this thing!" Her support meant a great deal. The Outward Bound property is isolated and the run was along rural country roads, so it was devoid of people. Her words of encouragement lifted me when I needed it most.

Reward: I have never used rewards in the conventional way – as in buy a new dress or go out somewhere. For me, the reward of achieving my goals was the internal satisfaction of having completed the project. The real reward is the break following the goal from the relentless focus! However you do it, savouring success is a key part of the true grit challenge.

I invite you to undertake your own true grit challenge

Choose a 30-day, 90-day, or 1-year true grit challenge. Use the lists below to spark some ideas!

Personal challenges:

- 30 days of no coffee
- 30-day diet cleanse
- 90-day book writing challenge.

Or try a Physical true grit challenge:

- Body building/bikini contest
- Marathon or triathlon
- Climb a peak – Mt Kilimanjaro
- 100 push-ups in a row
- 100km walk.

Professional true grit ideas:

- Apply for a new job with greater responsibilities
- Learn a new skill like coding
- Volunteer to lead a new team.

Try a mindset true grit challenge

Courage: Do something that scares you, like public speaking or doing a stand-up comedy routine; do something different each day. Learning: learn a new language, travel to a new country, join a new social group. Put yourself out there!

Go for it. Strength is built under pressure, and we can withstand more than we know. We can build our capacity to survive crucibles by creating our own true grit experiences. Through dis-equilibrium we grow; with true grit we transform.

Threats to true grit: How not to beat yourself up

"You idiot!" I berated myself for locking the car before taking my bag out. I was in a flap, rushing to an appointment. That morning I had dropped a picture and cracked the glass, dumped half the chicken food bucket over my feet, and slipped, taking the stairs two at a time.

Breathe.

Calling myself an idiot was not going to help. I remember that my mentor Peter Cook took an oath of kindness as a modern-day meditation monk. The oath was never to say an unkind word, including to oneself. I like this oath and have adopted it as a principle by which to live.

Crap. Here I was, beating myself up. Oath failure. That just made me feel worse. Double oath failure.

It got me thinking about the true grit challenges I explored with my 'Leadership Over Lunch' group. True grit challenges to develop resolve and resilience need to be hard. They must cause dis-equilibrium, and call us to grow. Each of these challenges are noble in the intended outcome. Test limits, expand connection capacity, fine-tune digestive system.

If they are done as a punishment, they do not serve us. If we have the mindset of, "I'm not good enough yet, therefore I will do this challenge to make me better", then this is self-sabotage and self-deprecation. We are hurting ourselves with judgement.

Choosing a challenge should be an investment in growth, not a punishment for deficits.

Frankly, the thought of running another marathon feels like punishment to me. I won't grow with that as a challenge, noble as it is. I already know I can run marathons; I have completed six; I don't need to stretch myself that way anymore.

The true grit challenge I will undertake is of radical compassion – for myself. I have committed to 30 days of compassion: no swearing at, name-calling, or denigrating myself. I'm strengthening boundaries with my time and relationships. I'm not doing anything out of duty, obligation, or 'should'. I'm honouring my sleep time and nurturing my body with healthy food choices. I'm investing in self-awareness with daily shadow integration work, as per Ken Wilber et al in *Integral Life Practice* [30] (a fabulous book for all leaders called to evolve their thinking and being).

This true grit challenge feels harder than any other. Why is it harder to love ourselves than to criticise?

If we are going to develop our voice to be truth-tellers, then we need to start by being truthful with ourselves. Being able to speak hard truths needs a strong heart. Radical compassion is my commitment to get there.

What 30 day true grit challenge will you commit to? How will you grow through it? Who will you become as a result?

Key takeaways

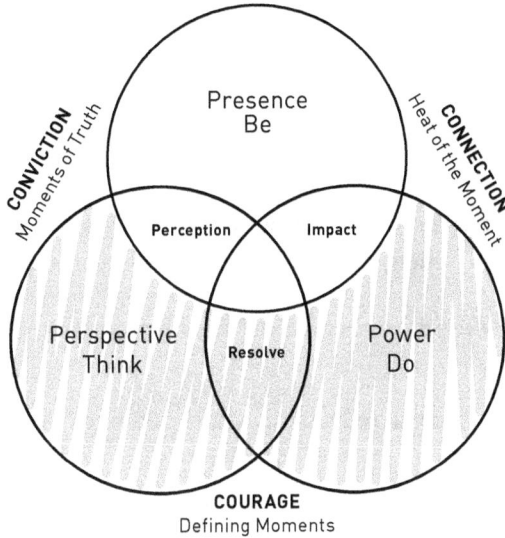

CONVICTION
Moments of Truth

CONNECTION
Heat of the Moment

Presence
Be

Perception

Impact

Perspective
Think

Resolve

Power
Do

COURAGE
Defining Moments

Perspective is the key to difficult decisions. We need to reflect deeply to know our own best path forward. No action gets taken until we develop personal *power*. A strong sense of identity and well-maintained boundaries shores up our power. True grit is what gives us the energy for *resolve*. In our resolve we find the *courage* to act when it is easier not to.

In defining moments where your credibility and reputation are at stake, finding perspective requires grounding in key principles

- Each person has their own truth. As leader, you need to hear them all in order to build buy in.
- Delivering bad or difficult news can be delivered with kindness and an invitation rather than as a directive.
- Be mindful to be 'I' focused instead of 'we' focused.

Perspective is needed for the most difficult choices, the 'rock and hard place' moments.

Put decisions through the Meaning – Magnitude – Measure framework

- Assess **Meaning**: Consequences for self, others, and the organisation/community/planet

- Assess **Magnitude**: Consequences if everyone made the same choice

- Assess **Measure**: Alignment with personal values, balance of harm versus benefit, alignment against universal principles.

Power is exercised when we run our choices through the choice filters

- **Define**: The choice reflects my character – am I comfortable with that?

- **Decide**: Am I prepared to accept the consequences?

- **Deliver**: Make the decision being prepared to process all emotions – success, shame, guilt.

Power is developed by developing the Character Castle

- **Construct** a solid personal identity and a useful definition of success

- **Craft** a strong physicality/ self-care and self-talk

- **Collect** compliments, results, and evidence of your awesomeness – the 'Nice Things' folder.

Power is protected by building the 'boundaries moat'

Know what you are prepared to accept and what you are not. Ask and expect these boundaries to be honoured.

Beware of where we can erode our personal power

- **Deflection**: Rejecting or discarding compliments and appreciation

- **Denigration**: Poor self-talk where we put ourselves down

- **Dissolution**: Self-sacrifice that turns us into victims unnecessarily.

Develop edgy personal power by honing true grit

Undertake a true grit project each 30 or 90 days, or even a 12-month true grit project. True grit projects are an investment in growth, not a punishment for deficits.

— ¤ —

Courage is what we find in defining moments. It helps us find the energy and resilience to be seen, heard, and as a result, valued.

PART FOUR

Heat of the Moment (Interpersonal)

26. About the heat of the moment

The truth-teller's guide to developing impact

When we have deep centered presence and the grit of deep personal power, we show up strong and engaging. We can stand our ground without blocking people. We manage our own emotions and help others to do the same in high stakes conversations. This is it. This is where we show up and handle the most challenging of all moments with others. We either deliver, or find ourselves wanting. We connect, or mis-hit.

The heat of the moment is when we are triggered emotionally. Biologically, our survival mechanism is activated, and we deploy our flight, fight, or freeze response to ensure our survival. This is our amygdala taking over the executive functions of our brain. It sends messages to release adrenaline and cortisol to our system to boost our physical strength, and prepares us for the fight or the run. When this happens, the rational part of our brain is short-circuited. We can't learn, we can't collaborate, and our short-term memory recall is affected. It's not good for connection: we are a ball of burning angst.

When we are in a tough conversation and our amygdala is triggered, this is when we might find ourselves blowing up or shutting down. This is when the impact does the most damage to our reputation, relationships, and influence.

What we need is Emotional Aikido, which I discussed briefly in *Composure*. Emotional Aikido is the ability to disarm our own emotional triggers and avoid those of others in a tough conversation. We can also protect ourselves and others when things heat up. It disables the threat without doing further harm, just as they teach in the physical martial art practice.

27. The rules of engagement

Leaders today exist in a difficult paradox. The leadership contract of millennia still weaves the threads of our tribal consciousness; the leader still protects and directs the tribe. There is an expectation that the leader will go to bat for us, will stand up for us, will speak out for us. And yet we always expect leaders to listen. We want them to consult, to be collaborative, be democratic, and to search for consensus where possible.

If the leader draws a line in the sand and makes a decision, they are rebuffed as an egomaniac tyrant. We feel disappointed that our advice, our thoughts, our ideas aren't adopted. We have moved from the joy of being consulted to the expectation that this means all our ideas are implemented. In fact, we have come to see ourselves as the real leaders, worthy of due regard. We have let slip the need for deference to authority.

I have found that best way to combat disappointment from team members is to connect, to ask questions, and to genuinely hear the response. Many leaders do this poorly. If they do consult they will throw a question out to test the waters. Those who are forceful or quick enough will spout their opinion, while others who need time to gather their thoughts are left scrambling for a voice.

I sat seething in a meeting recently. Everything was irritating for me. The meeting was a deluge of information updates. What a time-waster! We could have received that information in dot points prior to the meeting. So when it came time to discuss my proposal on a potential strategic initiative, we were cramped for time. That was the first irritation.

The second irritation came after I presented the issue for discussion. The chair immediately jumped in with her objections, effectively shutting down discourse. I tried to rescue the conversation by deliberately asking each of my other colleagues their respective opinions. In other words, doing what the chair should have done: canvas all opinions before making a ruling on the topic.

In the end, I was pissed off. My idea had been squashed without due exploration, and the chair pushed her own perspective on the group before even seeking consultation from others. Bahhhh!

The leader has to balance the fine line between being consultative and being decisive.

We do this through connection. Asking each person their opinion, listening to the perspective, and summarising at the end to demonstrate understanding is the simplest and easiest way to show connection. If this had happened in that meeting, I would have felt far better about the outcome, even if it didn't go in my favour. I might have listened more effectively to my colleagues as they voiced their opinions – for or against – knowing each were given an opportunity to share perspective. I would have felt heard. This is also how we know that we are not dealing with a tyrant, an egomaniac, someone in service to their own agenda. This is the critical moment in leadership connection where the leader must bridge consultation and decision-making.

Rules of engagement to consider

To avoid moments where people are triggered and emotional, there are some structural things we can do as leaders. If we are going to encourage connection and collaboration, we need some ground rules. These are shared expectations of how the team will operate together. Some common and useful ones are:

- Everyone's opinion is equal and has a right to be shared.
- Do not interrupt while someone else is talking.
- Membership of the group is non-negotiable, except in the case of gross misconduct such as assault, bullying, or harassment.
- Meetings will start and finish on time, with an agenda circulated ahead of time.
- Meetings will be for decisions or for ideas sharing. The meeting agenda will be clear ahead of time as to the purpose and outcome required.
- If you have a concern or issue with someone, address it in person and not over email.

Process and structure for teams to develop

- **Roles:** Role clarity is incredibly important. This helps avoid any territory disputes. With newer teams, this may take a few weeks to sort out as new processes and new decisions arise. Working collaboratively and openly on roles will help develop the best system so that all the right stakeholders are informed through the process. Document these so there is a reference point and manual for later. Processes evolve, so the manuals may need to be updated.

- **Decisions:** Develop clarity around what gets accepted, what gets rejected, and why. These are guidelines for decision-making. Document the process.

- **Delegation:** Get clear about who does what, and why.

- **Deputation:** Get clear about who steps in for the leader, and why.

- **Feedback:** Develop clear guidelines for how feedback is delivered, and expectations on how it will be processed, both individually and as a team.

- **Disagreements:** Develop a clear and documented process for handling disagreements at an individual and team level.

- **Failure:** Celebrate and learn from failures regularly. Be the first to admit mistakes, what you learned, and what you will do in the future.

28. How to avoid being a tyrant, or a hero

We are struggling under the weight of old leadership paradigms. The old reliance on the hero who cries, "Listen to me, follow me, believe me". It's the kind of leadership resolve that needs to be re-vamped. This section explores the pitfalls of the hero paradigm and makes the case for the 'hero leader' as someone who creates a team of heroes. This is reinvention of leadership through moments of questions, collaboration and connection.

We want to believe in the hero. We want to believe that Luke Skywalker can save the Galaxy and restore balance to the Force. We want to believe that there are courageous, risk-all folks who will battle through despite the odds to save the day.

My favourite story growing up was of King Arthur and the Knights of the Round Table.

I loved this story because it showed a decent man, one of deep values, of humility, who honoured the skills and attributes of his individual knights. And he had a *round* table. This was a symbol that all knights were equal, though each was different in his kingdom. Allegedly he did this to prevent disputes between his barons, who did not want to be placed lower in rank at the traditional rectangular table. King Arthur's Round Table equalised the sense of importance of each contributor.

This idea of the 'round robin', each person given the floor to share their opinion, harks back to this notion. Everyone gets an equal say. And King Arthur's method is the most under-utilised in leadership meetings. Most meetings are a free-for-all in discussions, or dominated by one or two hogs.

The chivalrous code was another tribute of the Round Table. It was meant as a moral guideline and honour code on the expected proper of the knights: to show mercy, to be respectful of gentlewomen, to show bravery, courtesy, honour, and great gallantry toward women. The codes of chivalry also incorporated the notion of courtly love.

Modern-day codes exist in other military bands, such as the Navy SEALs. The SEAL Code serves as a remarkable benchmark:

- Loyalty to Country, Team and Teammate
- Serve with Honor and Integrity On and Off the Battlefield
- Ready to Lead, Ready to Follow, Never Quit
- Take Responsibility for your Actions and the Actions of your Teammates

- Excel as Warriors through Discipline and Innovation
- Train for War, Fight to Win, Defeat our Nation's Enemies
- Earn your Trident everyday.

It's a pretty intense list, and is designed to galvanise its members for enormous feats of courage in difficult circumstances. The contemporary corporate list of 'Values and Code of Conduct' is an attempt to create a similar ethos in the business world.

But these corporate creeds often fail, or end up as a poster stuck on a wall and ignored. The SEAL code is embedded with expected behaviours, not just a list of values. Most corporate organisations have no such list of defined behaviours.

At a recent executive retreat, we started the discussion about ground rules for the team. The first suggestion was, 'respect each other's differences'. When I probed them to be more specific, to identify what they would see or hear if people were respecting each other's differences, we drilled down to these:

- Use 'yes and... ' to agree instead of 'yes but... '.
- If there are tensions, raise them with the other person.
- If there are tensions in the meeting, press pause on the conversation by using the phrase, "Excuse me, can we address something here. The story I am telling about this issue is…" This is what Brené Brown advocates using as a cut through sentence.
- To start every meeting, to get a mood check on the group from the outset, the team members each share an "I am ... " statement. They can summarise their current situation, share how they are feeling with "I am feeling elated / disappointed / frustrated", and then identify what they are going to do about it, if anything.

I find this last strategy a remarkably useful way to get insight into what emotions are in the room, what issues are hiding under the surface, and what else may be at play in the meeting. It allows us to go a little under the surface of observable behaviours from the outset to diffuse any tensions up front before they escalate unnecessarily.

How the leader can avoid being the tyrant and diffuse the need to be the hero

In this engagement with their executive team, the leader takes on the role of sage and compassionate coach, listener, and facilitator.

At the end of the day, the leader is to make decisions on behalf of the group, even if the group does not agree fully. For leaders to hear each team member fully diffuses tension, and leads to respect for the leader and the team process as a whole. In this way, if the team member doesn't get their way, this does not mean they are dismissed or ignored. It's a fine tension for the leader to manage: of listening, hearing, acknowledging, and sometimes disagreeing, and making decisions that do not always align with the team members' desires or opinions.

The leader must bring his or her band of knights to the table. The leader must keep them anchored to the bigger purpose and remind them it's about what they serve, not their own ideas.

If the leader does make a decision that goes against what the group wants, and that decision ends up in a failure, then there is risk here for the team to default to "We told you so." And thereby undermine confidence and faith in the leader. What we do here is admit the mistake and do a post-mortem on what went wrong, owning our role in the mess. By admitting failure and determining that some good can come of it through learning, we model the ability to take risks, fail, and learn. This kind of experimentation is what we need in leaders and teams.

If we have consulted well, heard well, and aggregated opinions, gently laid some ideas aside with what looked like good reasons at the time, and if we fail then admit our mistakes, then the team is more likely to go with us. We were transparent in our decision-making process, thorough in our consideration, and humble in our learning. This kind of behaviour shows respect for others.

It's a King Arthur model of heroism. His deep respect for his knights and his celebration of their individual achievements as well as their collective mission earned him the deepest respect of all.

The hero leader needs a reinvention. Ultimately we want a hero leader who can cultivate the strengths of their individual 'knights', invite them to the table as equals, and wear the burden and privilege of speaking for them, and of making decisions and ultimately accepting responsibility on their behalf. The hero leader is not saving the day on their own, but working with their team to save the day. The hero leader is really a leader of heroes. To cultivate heroism in our team is the true mandate of the modern leader.

29. How to cultivate heroism

Cultivating heroism is a fine tension between rallying around the mission and purpose, and celebrating the achievements of the individual. Recognition is a deep need for us as individuals. It boosts the feel-good hormone serotonin and satisfies the other feel-good hormone, dopamine – the hormone of achievement.

To be singled out for a job well done give us a sense of warmth and appreciation. To be part of a high-performing tribe or team fuels another hormone – oxytocin. That deep sense of trust and belongingness is a deep need for us as humans, and is one that has been around since we crawled out of the mud to set up camp on land. Belonging is what keeps us surviving, and enjoying the ride.

Kevin Rudd: when it all goes pear shaped

Former Australian Prime Minister Kevin Rudd has a reputation for many things. His campaign slogan 'Kevin '07' soon morphed in to 'Kevin 24/7' when he became Prime Minister. He became well-known for his relentless work ethic, and the high expectations he had of his staff.

Staff turnover in his office was listed at 40 per cent in the first 12 months of him taking office. Rudd was known as the toughest boss in Australia. Clearly, something was not working properly. Rudd was known to fly off the handle at a moment's notice. He littered his conversations with the F-bomb and even the C-bomb. He kicked a hole in the wall of his own office, and punched the wall of a plane following critical comments of his appearance after a UN address.

One news article reported from a staff member:

> "Kevin Rudd's work pattern was erratic. He would push himself to the limit. Convinced he needed little sleep, almost seeing this as a badge of honour. But he would get over-tired, his temper would fray, then he would need a day's break to recover... Kevin thrived on the sense of crisis, the 24-hour media cycle, requests for immediate advice, urgent phone calls and briefings. The GFC decision-making format came to define the government permanently. We never reverted to orthodox decision-making." [31]

The recipients of his vitriol extended beyond his immediate circles. On one occasion he lost his temper when his meal request on a flight was not fulfilled. He exchanged heated words with a 23-year-old flight attendant who ended up in tears. He apologised to her, and also in public, to the media.

We all have bad days. We can make mistakes. Sometimes we say things we do not mean and deeply regret. These are rare occasions. If the behaviour is chronic and rests with the most senior leadership position of a nation (who can make life and death decisions about going to war at a moment's notice), is this acceptable?

There are a number of key learning points from this very public example of how not to behave:

- If you are running in crisis mode all the time, things are bound to snap. Chronic adrenaline and cortisol lead to frayed tempers and compromised immune systems.

- Avoid the hero/rescuer/tyrant complex. The world will not fall apart if you have a bad day or have a poor performance. Your team is there to help your objective, not hinder. And the objective (especially as Prime Minister!) is a collective one, not a personal one. Your job title is not your persona; it's a responsibility.

- Learn to master emotions. See Part 2 and how to deal with rock bottom moments and letting your feelings be your teachers.

· Peak performance needs primary attention to your personal energy systems. I wrote about this extensively in Composure, and earlier in this book. Since we are bio-chemical soups, we need to make sure we manage our physical energy well with appropriate nutrition, sleep, exercise, rest, and hydration.

30. Emotional Aikido

Emotional Aikido requires training and execution of the learned skills, just like any athlete. It consists of two parts:

1. Physical training

2. Intention training.

Execution of Emotional Aikido in the moments that matter requires both awareness and action.

Physical training

Any athlete trains extensively, hour after hour, for the occasion of a combat, be it a race, a competition, or an incident that requires quick response.

If you remember *Karate Kid* (both the 1984 original and the 2010 re-make), Mr Miyagi's first training exercise with his impatient student is to paint the fence. In the re-make, Jayden Smith is made to put on and take off a jacket. Both complain that this has nothing to do with training for karate. After many days and hours, all is revealed. The exercise is to build muscle memory and instinct in defence modes. Paint the fence and the jacket on-off become the moves required to block an attack. The young Daniel, and Dre in the re-make, have built sufficient muscle memory that these moves are now instinctive.

This same principle applies to Emotional Aikido training. We must undertake daily, banal activities so that we can perform under pressure in a natural, instinctive way.

Train, don't drain with physical training

Physical training is designed to boost energy reserves and keep them at optimum levels. One of Kevin Rudd's faults was that he drained his energy tank and became reactive instead of responsive.

- **Exercise:** This needs a balance of exertion and recovery, both during workouts and between workouts.

- **Nutrition:** The fundamentals apply. Eat mostly what builds and supports you (whole foods) and less of what drains you (processed foods, sugar).

- **Hydration:** Drink more of what hydrates you (water, herbal teas) and less of what taxes you (alcohol, caffeine, sugary juices and drinks).

- **Sleep:** Undertake effective sleep hygiene habits. Sleep in a cold room. Shut down electronics at least an hour before bed. Use blue light blocking glasses if you are using screens after dark. Get out in the sun each day for 20 minutes.

- **Recovery:** Rest is crucial. Take frequent mini-beaks during the day. Book in a day off each week. A full weekend each month with no work. A holiday each year.

- **Breath control:** All military training includes some form of breath control for a good reason. It helps regulate cortisol and heart rate. Deep breathing activates the rest and digestive system and calms us down. Practice taking three deep breaths in the morning, at lunch, and before bed, and whenever you feel anxiety rising.

- **Pose:** Do the Wonder Woman/Superman pose of hands on hips for two minutes each day to lower cortisol and boost testosterone. This will make you feel more confident, as well as appear more confident. Amy Cuddy has a great TED talk on this and her new book goes in to greater detail.[32]

Intuition training

Intuition is a renewable energy source. Tap the bottomless well, as your intuitive energy is always available. The trick is learning how to access it at will.

Develop your intuition with small things: Use the small decisions to go with an impulse, like what colour underpants, what meal to eat, which way to work. When you consciously practice going with your instinct, you begin to trust your intuition more, and can use it for more significant decisions.

Journal: Use a journal to process your experiences. Reflect on your achievements, feelings, and insights. You will soon develop greater self-awareness, which will help in more challenging moments.

Action review: Use your journal for positive action review. Examine what went well, what could improve, and ask what you are grateful for.

Insight

In 2000, I realised it was time to make good on a promise I had made to myself when I was only 10. My Dad had run a few marathons, and I always watched him excitedly as he ran past in the race, with a big grin on his face. I thought to myself: "I'm going to run a marathon by the time I'm thirty."

At the age of ten, 30 was a long way off, so there was no pressure. So I ignored and avoided that intention until in 2000 when it was "now or never". I bought the most useful book I could find, *The Non-Runner's Marathon Trainer*,[33] and started following its training regime. The furthest I had run, ever, was 10km. I was not a runner. I knew nothing of the sport or the process or what to expect.

On the other side of the world, my sister was inspired by my declaration. She would run the marathon with me, and make a holiday of it.

My sister's intention was much different to my own. The previous year her former partner, a disturbed and unhappy young man, had instigated a reconciliation with my sister. He was a well-regarded

Michelin Star chef. Their breakup had been traumatic, as he was immersed in drug addiction brought on by bipolar disorder that stemmed from the incomprehensible black pain at the hands of his own mother. He was a troubled man, but he was trying to make good. He talked of marriage and babies, and my sister wanted to believe.

Then she got the call telling her Nicolas was found dead, having hung himself in his own restaurant. She was devastated. We all were.

So she decided to train and run a marathon with me, as a way of processing her grief. She trained all through the wet, bitter Montreal winter, inside on a treadmill. Some of the long training runs were over three hours. On a treadmill.

How can intention be a powerful force?

When it resonates deeply with us, intention can bring us through arduous circumstances. Everything in our lives is better with strong intentions. Consider the experience of going to the gym. Some go to 'work out'. They sit on an exercise bike with a trashy magazine propped up on the handlebars. They are completely disassociated from their body.

Others treat their time at the gym as a sacred focus on self-development. Their intention is not to 'work out' but to train. They are training their mind-body connection, their focus, and the intention in improving aspects of their fitness on that day. This might be flexibility, strength, endurance, stamina, and power. There are oodles of studies that have quantified the effect of deliberate focus and intention on specific, measurable results, including increase in muscle mass and reduced stress hormone results.

In other words, when we focus with intention, good things happen.

When we focus on others, our thoughts have an impact on us as well as on them. If we choose our thoughts with a positive intention, we can create positive interaction with others.

Practical examples of how thought affects form

Plants responding to the intention effect

Lynne McTaggart explores this phenomenon in *The Intention Experiment* (2007). Her first experiments were on plants.[34] She measured the impact of messages spoken to plants by photographing their leaves and seeing the electromagnetic frequencies emitted as a result. Some plants were spoken to lovingly, and some were threatened with nasty messages such as, "I'm going to burn your leaves you rotten little mongrel." It turns out that the plants that received loving messages thrived under the attention, and those who were threatened emitted an electromagnetic threat response. The plants understand, in their plant consciousness, when they were under threat, or being supported.

Cool, huh?

McTaggart's next experiments explored the power of focused intention from a distance. The implications were tantalising. The power of thought was real and measurable. She ran many different experiments testing the power of intention and focused intention from a distance too. Distance had no impact. No matter where her meditators were and where the intended object or person was, there was a measurable impact. Lynne extended her experiments to global peace experiments.

When we focus our intention we can shift the physical world. This is also how the power of prayer operates, and why talking to plants has always been seen as a good idea. Plants, like people and animals, respond well to attention.

Masaru Emoto's water crystal photographs

Researcher Masaru Emoto[35] photographed water crystals after bombarding them with different verbal messages, such as 'love', 'hate', 'war', and 'friends'. The results were intriguing. The positive words resulted in well-formed, symmetrical shapes. The negative words created misshapen and broken crystals.

We can imagine that negative and harmful words – whether from ourselves or others – would have the same effect on the water in our cells. Our body is made up of 70 per cent water, so this is a serious effect. The question is, what does this mean for our health? For our wellbeing?

The inference, whether you believe the experiment or not, is that positive words are likely to be more helpful than negative ones. Our thoughts and emotions have a real, visceral, cellular impact. Positive, compassionate words comfort and heal; negative words and insults hurt. So if we are going to be interacting with folks, we need to be deliberate and careful with this.

Unbendable arm in Aikido

One of the key premises of the martial art Aikido is managing chi, or energy. The first exercise that people undertake is 'unbendable arm'. You must visualise energy shooting out from your arm, as through a firehose. It renders your arm strong and unbendable, rather than relying on muscular strength alone.

In our lives, when you focus through with an intention, your physical being relaxes, and you are more centered. When you are centered, you can respond rather than react to circumstances, staying in control and able to direct the flow of conversation. When you resist or try to fight, you are actually weaker and are able to be pushed around by others.

David Hawkins: Power vs force

Philosopher David Hawkins measured the frequency output of individuals in various different emotional states. The testing method is from kinesiology. This is the practice of testing physical response to questions / ideas / emotions through muscle testing. David Hawkins tested people's response in emotional states and then ranked them from more powerful to less powerful.

From this we learn that different emotional states make us feel more or less powerful or strong. Anger, guilt, and shame are not that powerful. Appreciation, courage, joy are very powerful. You shift to higher emotional states through the practice of appreciation. It's like a micro-gear shifter. Appreciation brings the feeling of relief to the current emotional state, and then you can move your way up the scale. Neuroscience shows us that positive moods are more contagious than bad moods. The exception is the boss's mood. Because of our natural deference to our leaders, the leader's mood is more influential: bad moods radiate more from leaders, and so do good moods.

Key tips for intention hygiene

- **Self, them, world**
  Constructive, growth, connected conversations have these three aspects of intentions in them.

- **Beware vagueness**
  Vagueness can be superficial and full of platitudes. You have to be genuine about why you want to engage and what the relationship is all about.

- **Beware conflicting intention**
  Not having the conversation may meet another need, such as the need for belongingness, acceptance, or compliance.

- **Beware of hidden payoffs**
  Selfish intentions can be masked with good intentions.

- **Cognitive bias skews**
  Intention might be filtered by frames like the halo effect. Dr Jason Fox lists a dozen or more in his book *How to Lead a Quest* (2015).[36]

- **Attention Out**
  Being in service to others is like unbendable arm: you relax, and you send out good energy.

Intention questions to ask:

- Who are they?
- What is important to them?
- What are they interested in?
- What is at stake for them?
- What is their behaviour preference?
- What does an ideal outcome look like to them?

Think: "Just like me, they ..."

- have dreams

- have people they care about

- are doing their best.

Intention checklist:

- Is your intention honourable?

- Is your intention clear?

- Do you have conflicting intentions?

- Do you have other un-met needs?

- Does this serve me?

- Does this serve other/s?

- Does this serve the world and humanity?

31. Awareness in the heat of the moment

I have a confession: I love martial arts movies. The focus and energy required to pull off amazing feats is remarkable. The films are a testament to the power of focus and will. If we are in the heat of the moment, we need this kind of deep awareness that martial artists possess of the immediate moment in order to respond, and not react to the challenges.

There are five ways we can develop this awareness in the heat of the moment.

1. Know thyself

Awareness in the moment begins with paying attention.

Take a moment. Where are you right now? What is going on around you? Are you alone, or are there people there? Noisy or quiet? Music or silence? Do colours predominate? Background noises? What is the air quality like: hot, cool, stuffy, fresh?

Turn inwards: what do you feel right now? What do you notice about how you feel immersed in the environment? What about your thoughts? Are they jumbled? Is your mind racing ahead? Are you doing something else apart from reading this? What is your inner world like?

As we saw previously, our thoughts have an impact on our bodies and on the people and things around us. Do you notice what you are broadcasting? Taking stock of what you are experiencing in the moment is the art of mindfulness, and is the key to acute and grounded presence.

2. Be aware of how the environment affects you

Environment directs and distracts our mood and focus.

We project out on the environment just as we receive broadcasts from it, much like a two-way walkie-talkie. We've got to learn to send and receive with our surroundings.

The environment actually forms an integral character in the 1957 movie *12 Angry Men*.

The film is set in a New York City courthouse in the height of summer. The jury is instructed to deliberate on whether an 18-year-old boy is guilty of murdering his father in one of the city slums. A guilty verdict brings a mandatory death penalty sentence. The circumstantial evidence seems to support the hypothesis that the boy did it. Coupled with the oppressive heat in a small, stuffy room, the pressure to solve the verdict quickly mounts. There is only one juror who hesitates to declare 'guilty'. The jury dig in to work their way through the evidence. One by one, after tempers and frustration grate at one another, they explore the assumptions that had supported an easy guilty verdict. The heat turns up the heat, so to speak.

Environment can also dictate a whole community's approach to social interactions.

In the Torres Strait in the warm tropics north of Cairns, Australia, the temperature varies little from 25 degrees Celsius. They have a distinct approach to managing activities, which is known as 'island time'. Island time means that things will happen in their own time, at the right time. Adhering to rigid schedules is foreign and out of place. It's a very relaxed approach to life. This is found elsewhere in hot, tropical areas around the world.

I grew up in Canada and this ethos definitely did not exist! As summer is so fleeting, there is a sense of urgency and energy when the seasons change. There is a rush to garden, to exercise, to throw off the winter layers and let our pasty winter skin soak up some summer sunshine. There is no time to go with the flow! We behave differently in different climates.

Environment creates outlooks from a meta-perspective, as well as a micro perspective.

A room can inspire or unnerve. A building can generate feelings of being trapped or feelings of grandeur. Human beings have long known the power of a building to inspire or intimidate. Cathedrals celebrate the wonder of the divinity, creating spaces of awe and beauty to direct human thoughts to the ethereal and spiritual. Prisons, in contrast, do no such thing. I wonder if prisons were designed as cathedrals, what kind of impact this might have on rehabilitation. The most progress we see is in painting walls pink. This is allegedly to keep prisoners docile and obedient.

Deliberately crafting an environment that stimulates thinking, or calms the nerves, or is warm and inviting, is a useful strategy for leaders who want to match their environment to their intention. Everything in our environment has an energetic quality to it, and affects us when we are in the vicinity. To master ourselves, it's useful to know how we feel and react in different environments. It's likely you already know what kind of natural environment you prefer: mountains or sea? Country or city? Garden or gallery?

The next level of awareness is noticing your internal world as you more through different external worlds. Tune in to yourself when you go to your garage, your car, the supermarket, the shopping mall. Notice what upsets you, irritates you, or uplifts you. Just pay attention to your internal chemistry.

Notice how you feel around other people too. Some people may make you feel at ease, warm, happy, and others may cause you to withdraw, others to anger. Just note what is going on around and with the other person or people that create a reaction in you.

As I described in my first book, *Composure*, you can then start to enact energetic protection so you can feel less buffeted by people and things around you. By imaging the shape of an octahedron around you, for instance, you can reclaim your dispersed energy. You can let go of any energy that does not support you, and keep other people's vibes from affecting you. This is very useful in tense meetings, delivering feedback, having conversations when the stakes are high, or even when you feel nervous yourself.

In our most important discussions with others, we need to:

· Set the scene.

· Choose the environment.

· Notice what affects us (temperature, colour, noise, sound) and manage the effects as best as possible.

3. Awareness creates perfect timing

When we are hyper focused, we can anticipate. The world seems to slow down a little and we can appear to have supernatural senses. I love watching tennis great Roger Federer for this reason. When he is in form, he is super focused and detached. His attention is on the movement of the ball and the gestures and micro-movements of his opponent, so he can anticipate where the ball will land with masterful precision. In some slow-motion reviews, we can see he actually closes his eyes on many strokes, just before the moment of impact.

In many martial arts movies, when the novice is being trained by a master practitioner, we often hear the teacher say "use all your senses, stretch out perception beyond the physical". This was Obi-Wan Kenobi's first instruction to Luke: "Reach out with your feelings".

Aside from popular culture, we often hear about this kind of exercise in meditation and spiritual practices. It helps us tune in to our environment and sense beyond what is visible. This is the development of intuition. It starts with awareness of surroundings, awareness of internal responses, then deliberately reaching out with imagination to feel what is going on elsewhere.

Body scan

One of my favourite intuition development exercises is using the imagination to scan through the body, eyes closed. The next stage is to imagine my awareness expanding to include the room I am in. Then the building, then the street, the neighbourhood, the city, the country, the globe, and outward in to the galaxy and across the universe. It is incredibly calming, and heightens sensory awareness.

4. Our biochemical soup can distort, or support

Our chemical body distorts perceptions. Becoming more aware of our body processes helps us to know when we are being coloured by our physiology. What we eat, what we drink, and how much we rest and sleep all affect our sensory instruments, hence our perception.

Like many people, when I get hungry it can quickly devolve into being 'hangry' (hungry and angry). This is the irritability that comes from the drop in blood sugar, the reduced cognitive function as my brain searches for absent glucose, and the slowing of its processes as it finds none. If not fed during the 'hangry' stage or before, my cognitive ability diminishes rapidly and I am unable to think a clear thought, respond quickly to questions, or make a decision. Unlike diabetics, however, my body self-regulates quickly with nourishment, whereas the diabetic may take some time to equalise blood sugars.

To master the moment, we need to master our body. Our body is a wonderful servant. When we master your body, we may also master our mind, and thus command the moment.

5. Posture presents

Our posture gives our inner world cues about what to do, how to feel, and broadcasts that outwards.

Nose, Toes, and Pose exercise

Nose: Breathe deeply to relax and activate the parasympathetic nervous system (rest and digest).

Toes: Dig your toes in to the floor. This will bring your focus in to your body, and in to the present moment – and out of the merry-go-round in your head.

Pose: These are using power poses (Wonder Woman and Superman) to promote positive relaxing chemicals in the body.

These 'nose, toes, and pose' cues calm us down, and they also signal subconsciously to others that we are calm and confident. This can help de-escalate tensions. If you appear confident, then you are not in 'fight' mode, and therefore there is no imminent threat to the other person. At least not from your body language.

Insight

"What are you going to do about it?" Tom was six foot three, and he towered over me with a sneer and squinted eyes.

"I paid for this program myself. That's ten thousand dollars out of my own pocket. I should be getting more for my money – this is crazy!" He stepped closer and looked down at me.

My heart pounded. I hate confrontation. He was accusing me and my colleagues of ripping him off, and for running a shoddy show. I was horrified to think he might think badly of me. My more immediate concern was the fact I felt cornered by this man. He was agitated, he was angry, and he was using his physicality to intimidate me. I knew I would go to my default of 'run away' if the sense of attack was not neutralised quickly.

I knew why Tom was upset. The start of experiential programs is deliberately confusing, ambiguous, and stressful. They are designed to put people under pressure, to push through conventional social politeness barriers so that people can quickly start having honest conversations. It's also an exercise in learning to speak the truth, in the heat of the moment, without dropping our bundle. For leaders who are used to being in control, to having all information at their fingertips, and being responsible for executing all plans, this exercise is incredibly destabilising. It is the state of being off balance that creates the opportunity for growth.

Tom was off-balance quickly and was going into survival mode. He lashed out at me to try and gain some control over what he perceived as an out-of-control situation. His default was clearly 'fight'. With me having a 'flight' default, this was not going to end in a satisfactory way for either of us, unless I did something to get us back on even and safe ground.

I initiated my most reliable Emotional Aikido move: I turned slightly outwards and invited him to walk with me. This had an immediate effect. It released the tension strung between us when he had stood face-to-face, standing over me like a Colossus.

We continued the conversation, and I listened to his concerns. These were mostly around feeling like he did not have enough food to perform well. His underlying worry was that he would not be able to engage effectively, and therefore be seen as a sub-performer. His reputation and ego felt threatened. I empathised, as I too get food stress. I felt compassion for him too: he just wanted to be thought well of by others. We came up with a compromise by adding some more food to the supplies and making sure there were adequate snacks for each activity.

Our learning outcomes maintained their integrity, and Tom maintained his dignity.

32. Overarching principles of Emotional Aikido

If we've done the training, we're ready. Through my engagement with Tom during the course, and though all of your 'heat of the moment' interactions, this is about *game on* – what you'll think, do, and be in the arena when the stakes are high.

Honour your opponent

See the divine in the other person. Alison and Darren Hill in *Dealing with the Tough Stuff* (2016) [37] say there is one key principle:

All people are good.

Think: "Just like me … they are doing their best, want happiness and a fulfilling life, have petty concerns, and big dreams." While people may behave badly, at their core essence, they are good. They are hoping to have a happy life, they want to do their best, and are likely trying their best (even if their best is dangerous).

This approach helps unhook from anger, bitterness, and frustration. I knew Tom was just trying his best. With time, I could see through his aggressive behaviour to what was driving it. There were good intentions there, buried behind poor behaviour.

Love bombs diffuse

Love bombs are simply sending positive thoughts and intentions to the other person or people.

- "I honour you as a fellow human being."
- "I may not like you or care for your views, yet I appreciate you as a human being."
- "I may not see how, but still I know you are trying your best."

As I talked with Tom, I silently sent him messages of approval that I cared for him as a human being, and that I respected his concerns.

Be safe

Safe conversations are where neither person has fallen into the amygdala trap. Be mindful of the signs of a hijack:

- **Flight:** Withdrawal, silence, leaving the room, and sarcasm. Sarcasm is a passive-aggressive flight manoeuvre.
- **Fight:** Insults, elevated voice, pointing, pushing one's agenda/opinion forcefully, anger, and aggressive body language.

Tom was in amygdala hijack mode. His arguments were circular, he was not listening to what I was saying, and he was using intimidating body language. I had to cut through this scenario by moving us physically first. This helped to calm the amygdala so we could talk rationally again. Sometimes we just need to take a break and call 'time out' so we can catch our breath and release the emotional tension.

Physicality matters

Manage your physicality to create an impact. Your posture gives important signals to others. As you enter a room and under a doorway, stand up tall and square your shoulders. You can pause for a brief moment to compose yourself and then make a deliberate entrance. This is how you embody your intention of confidence in your body language.

Mirror, don't mimic their body position

Body language dances happen naturally, once in rapport. You can initiate rapport by mirroring their body position. Sit like they are, put your arms on the table if they are, and lean in or out, depending on their posture. To get Tom back on safe ground and in rapport I had to break the tension first. I then asked him to sit so we could be at equal level.

Positioning

Be mindful of height, proximity, and your personal bubble, and create an escape valve (open space between you, with an angle outwards). With Tom, once we had sat down it was much easier. I could edge my chair as close as I could see he was comfortable. You'll notice someone's unconscious response to your proximity and learn when to lean in closer, and when to edge away.

Contact

A handshake, or touching the shoulder, builds a sense of connection and safety. Of course, be mindful of cultural taboos and protocols. When I got Tom to turn and walk, I put my arm lightly on his back as a gesture of reassurance and an invitation to walk. That small brief physical contact sent a message of safety and calm to him. It showed I still respected him, and trusted him to respond in a decent way.

Second circle energy

Be aware of your energy – which circle is it in? In *Presence* (2009),[38] Patsy Rodenberg talks about this from her experience as an actor. If you come in to a room very inwardly-focused, you are shrunken, reserved, and difficult to engage with (first circle). If you come into a room bouncing off the walls, you also push people away because you are over the top. You push your energy on to others (third circle).

Second circle energy– is where you are deeply centered, and you are open and attentive to others. It's a balance between attention *in* and attention *out*. Do this and you will be way more engaging with others.

When Tom stood over me, I recognised that I was shrinking into a submissive first circle, while he was in third circle. The imbalance was uncomfortable for both of us. So as I turned him aside to walk, I was able to think about him and to calm myself down, returning us both to second circle discussion.

Move and stop

If you want to draw attention to yourself and make people notice, move in to a room or space, and then stop. When I walked with Tom over to the chairs, I turned to him and stopped, looking him full in the face, then asked him to sit. I had his attention and it cut his panicked train of thought in its tracks.

Intake of breath

To get heard in a meeting, take a short intake of breath as if you were about to say something. People will turn to you then expectantly. Take this cue and say what you mean to say.

When Tom was getting carried away with his story of drama (another sign someone is about to get hijacked by their amygdala), I took a quick intake of breath, as if suddenly surprised by an idea. He stopped his own train of thought and asked me, "What is it?" I had successfully managed to cut his attention back to me, and out of his downward spiralling diatribe.

Lean in

This shows interest and engagement. Sheryl Sandberg named her book *Lean In* (2013) [39] for a reason. This move signals interest, engagement, presence and focus. It honours the conversation.

Belly breaths

Deep breaths calm you down. If you also observe other people breathing, it can act as a calming, centering technique as well. I had to take a few deep breaths when Tom first stood over me, and while we walked the short distance to the chairs. My head was screaming all sorts of insults and panicked thoughts, and I knew if I was going to salvage the situation, I had to run an intervention – on myself. Deep breaths to the rescue.

Matrix moves

Like in the movie *The Matrix* (1999), you may need to move out of the way of other people's energy. Energy can be turbulent and unsettling. So you can avoid it or deflect it. This does not have to be a huge martial arts move, but a simple shifting in your seat may be enough to avoid the energy.

With Tom standing over me, the Matrix move was turn and guide him to the seats. It cut off the power of his anger over me. I am always amazed about how shifting away from someone's energy fire can really make such a palpable difference in how comfortable we both feel.

Emotional Aikido: A summary

Keep a warm heart, cool head, and safe hands

Centered leaders who can respond with grace in any moment are known to have a calming presence that diffuses tension. You can feel their energy before you hear anything they say. Their warm heart is who they are: they hold positive good intentions for themselves and others as a key function of their being and leadership.

Centered leaders who can face any moment keep a cool head. They have mastered the art of feeling their emotions but not being driven by them. They can stand in the fury of the most extreme of circumstances and still function in a wise and compassionate way.

Centered leaders master their message. They screen their language and choose their words carefully so build rapport and connection. This is how they have safe hands. Their physicality also matters they are mindful of how to put others at ease, and how to command a space if needed.

As leader who can respond in any moment that matters, this is what you can do too. Build your emotional Aikido skills through daily practice. When the time comes when you are faced with a moment that seems insurmountable, you will find yourself poised and ready.

33. Being real

When I think about the moments that matter most in leadership, these are the moments when we need to be most fully ourselves. The moment when a colleague is having a meltdown. When our integrity is being challenged. When someone rejects our work. Our presence needs to be like a lightning bolt: bright, focused, electric. We need to be real.

Our presence – who we are – is the magic of our influence. Yes, we can learn some technical skills on being present, but nothing replaces the magic of you.

One thing that gets in the way of leaders being fully present is that we sometimes deny our bad bits. We try to make the right decisions, we try to behave the right way, and we try and suppress the nasty bits of us that don't seem so pretty. Those jealous, childish voices. Our criticisms of others. The judgements we make. The nasty, substandard habits. We might be a procrastinator, a hoarder, sloppy, with no attention to detail. We deny our lumps and bumps in the earnest effort to be better than who we are.

When we do this, those lumps and bumps grow to be volcanoes! The more we try to put a lid on it, the more it spills over. The trick to being whole and complete is making peace with and integrating those nasty lumps and bumps.

In Ken Wilber's *Integral Life Practice* (2012),[40] this is called shadow work. The shadow work exercise is to feel the feelings that we deny (the person that we try and avoid) and feeling that as a whole part of us. When we accept that we have the greatest good in us as well as the greatest evil, then we are not at the mercy of sudden eruptions. When we deny no part of ourselves, then we are complete. This is where we can disable the parts that might get us into trouble. We consciously choose which bits of us to act on, and which bits to keep dormant.

Compassion for ourselves means totally accepting all of who we are. It doesn't mean that we don't try to improve. It means that we seek to grow and evolve and let go of the things that no longer serve us without beating ourselves up. If we have a commitment to living a non-violent life, a compassionate life, then the magic of who we are evolves.

So I can show up and be all of me. Inside there is the Bitch, the Witch, and the Hag. There is also the Queen, the Crone, and the Muse. Through all of them there is Me. And I'm fine with that.

This is the essence of being *real*.

Key takeaways

Deep centered *presence* when combined with well-honed grit (*power*) and focus allows us to show up with impact, and create connection with others, even in the heat of the moment.

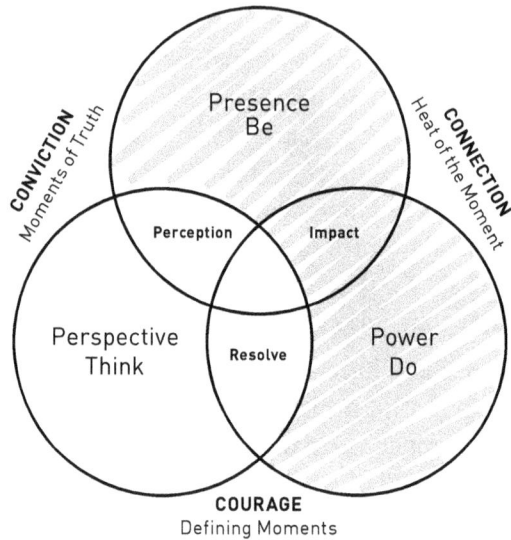

COURAGE
Defining Moments

When we cultivate our physical and intention training, we develop *presence*. We need to create processes to harness our *power* and those of others. We do this through good group structure. *Power* and *presence* creates *impact* – what we need for connection in the heat of the moment.

To prevent blowups:

· Develop rules of engagement

· Clarify roles, rules, decision making processes, disagreement procedures.

Cultivate heroism in your team members to avoid becoming a hero or tyrant.

Pressure and stress are no excuse for chronic aggressive or passive-aggressive behaviour. Get emotions and energy under control.

Emotional Aikido training includes:

· Do physical and intention training to harness your power and presence

· Developing a practice of 'intention hygiene' so you are expressing the best and highest version of yourself.

In the heat of the moment:

- Hone your awareness of self, others, and the environment
- Harness your ability to manage intention, message, and emotion while the pressure is on.

Practise these skills to show up with a warm heart, cool head, and safe hands

Our capacity to connect is the superpower that allows us to be seen, heard, and ultimately valued by others. When we show respect, when we act from positive intentions, people feel and appreciate us. Our intention becomes not to be seen, heard and valued, but to see, to hear, and to value.

Conclusion

34. Conviction, Courage, and Connection

If we are to be seen, heard, and valued, then it begins and ends with us. There is nothing more persuasive than someone who is anchored in their own conviction. This is the conviction that comes from moments of truth, when we discover our integrity.

Courage is built on personal power and perspective. Our conviction lets us know we can trust our inner compass, and shores up our courage. When we are courageous, we are compelling. There is nothing more encouraging than courage!

We make connections when courage and conviction come together with a clear attention on the moment, and the other person with us. It is a sacred moment where we can either connect, or mis-hit. Our ability to be attentive, truly listening, and truly engaged with another soul is the magic moment when we can either open possibilities or shut them down.

The irony is that in order to be seen, heard, and valued, our focus is not on trying to convince others of anything. When we discover our deep heart, we let go of any need to be seen, heard, and valued. We show up as authentic and compassionate. We are co-creators in a better world and honour the integrity and journey of the other person and other people around us. We have no need to convince, because we are here to explore together.

This is real leadership! We have dropped all facades, we have let go of any ego need to be recognised, and we stand knowing that the world is a better place because we have plumbed the depths of our own soul and have arisen with a fuller heart. This is what we bring to the table for influence: the brilliant lightning strike of pure authenticity. We light up the room with our character and our being. In doing so, we help others untangle their own struggles, and show them a path to be real.

Making the most of moments that matter comes down to a distillation of expansive leadership thinking, being, and doing into pure crystal resonance. When we have burned away all doubts and small inner voices, we have the capacity to be purely present and centered.

Listening to the unspoken voices

It takes courage and conviction to speak up and asked to be heard. Voice is a powerful emblem of identity and claiming our place in community.

Many of us feel marginalised and maligned. There are those in our community who do not feel their voice can or will be heard. Introverts struggle to contribute and cut through extroverted noise. Refugees labour to have their story understood, to explain what kind of terror could drive them to extreme lengths to escape their homeland and seek solace elsewhere. Transgender people experience the confusion and denigration each time they open their mouths and hear their voice contradict their identity: too deep to be a woman, too high-pitched to be a man. Their voice undermines their sense of self.

For a good century and more, we have been encouraging the voices of powerless minorities to speak up, to be seen and heard and taken into account. Suffragettes worked tirelessly for the right for women's voices to be taken into consideration on the political landscape. The right of ethnic minorities to be heard and seen and protected by law has been a critical progress in our social landscape.

In pointing out oppression, we have inadvertently disallowed some voices. Men are not allowed to talk of their concerns. They are often tarred with the blanket brush of the oppressive dominant majority.

Many would say that men do not need a voice, because they command the podium. They have rights, privilege and power that is embedded in conscious bias. We've all heard of the studies that showcase the blind favouritism towards male job candidates, even when two candidates were equally qualified, the male candidate was ranked higher. Why? Deep conscious bias that men are more competent, more reliable, or simply just better able to do the job? So with this working in men's favour, consciously and subconsciously, is there really a case to hear men's voices?

I believe there is. I believe the pendulum has swung far from center, and men are often held as the oppressors when they are not.

Many are desperately seeking to find their way in a new environment where their status as men is held in esteem as well as contempt. They are at risk of being accused of being sexist or racist. Much has been written on women's competing demands in the workplace and home, and next to nothing for what this means for men. Many men struggle with work and family duties, especially as expectations of them have grown too. They are no longer expected to be breadwinner, but also caregiver, and equal partner in household chores and romantic relationships. Where women have tried to work out how they juggle it all, men are simply expected to shoulder their fair share.

In reality, what happens is that men are expected to work, and then if their partner has a child, they are automatically rostered into primary breadwinner and secondary caregiver. Their lives become work, work, work, then take over duties at home. There is little left for exploring themselves as human beings afterwards. Men struggle to feel fulfilled, just like women.

The difference for men, however, is that they are not allowed to talk about it. It's akin to the derisive catch-cry, 'poor little rich boy'. By virtue of privilege it is then seen as improper or selfish to feel unhappy with one's lot. Suffering and pain, no matter its home, is still suffering and pain.

Where do men go to vent their emotions? Nowhere. Men are not encouraged to gather in their own space. Women's groups abound: in professional circles, in social circles, and in informal ones like mothers' groups. Men are left to connect with one another through an activity of some kind, like sport. Exclusive male circles are now taboo. The popular rise of Men's Sheds is a counterpoint to this trend. The Men's Shed movement evolved out of the recognition that men need space to be around other men where they are not judged and where they can share. Unfortunately some Men's Sheds have been pressured to make room for women.

By denying men's voices, we have been denying the richness of compassion that might come from embracing all perspectives: male, female, cross-gender, multicultural. We are all human. We have not achieved collaborative truth until all truths are allowed, shared, and explored.

Being able to exercise our voice matters. It is the one thing that makes it possible for us to lead effectively, with inspiration and conviction, in the moments that matter most. It is the pivot point in an opportunity made or an opportunity lost. Everything rides on our ability to sound our voice in the moment.

It is my hope that *Moments* helps you find your own inner voice and perspective, own all of who you are, and express that in a way that invites others to do the same. It means we need to make room for all voices and encourage them to be heard.

A life is a series of moments. Some heard and felt deeply, others missed and gone forever. The quality of attention we bring to moments is the quality of our life, in the end.

And what of the final moment? What of the moment when we leave our mortal coil behind? What meaning does this moment hold for us?

👁 Insight

In a literal 'bolt from the blue', a moment is all there is.

John squatted beside the tent, hammering a peg into the tough dry ground with a rock. It was lightly overcast. To the south there was a storm brewing with dark clouds, but it was moving north west of the camp and did not pose a direct threat. To the east the sky was clear.

There might be some rain so they were covering the tents. John stood to stretch his back.

The sky cracked and lightning seared the sky. The boom rocked the earth. Four others, just four metres away, were knocked to the ground. Reeling, they stumbled over to John. Amongst them was Kevin, the group leader.

The lightning had blown John's clothes clean from his body. He lay prone, eyes glassy, his naked body dimpling in the cold. Kevin reached over and squeezed John's shoulders, hard. No response. He had a faint pulse and had shallow breathing. His face was blue, his mouth frothing. Kevin placed him in the recovery position to clear his airway and monitor him while they waited for help. Thirty seconds later, he checked the carotid and radial artery. Nothing. Kevin started CPR. Another team member used the satellite phone to call emergency services.

Luck was with John that day. The group's resupply boat had left for its scheduled delivery just before the storm hit the lake. It bobbed up to shore just four minutes after Kevin started CPR. They received instructions from emergency services over the satellite phone. The operator guided them to cease CPR for ten seconds at a time while his peers moved him towards the boat on a makeshift stretcher. A couple of rounds of CPR, and then ten seconds to move. The scene was chaotic with John's friends calling out his name for support. The lift on to the boat was very difficult due to the waves which reached one to one and half metres. They manoeuvred him on to the boat and lay him across the supply boxes and cool boxes full of vegetables – no floor space was available.

Kevin continued CPR for 40 minutes while the tiny boat careened through the thrashing water, soaking them all. He tag teamed compressions with the group medic while another team member performed the assisted breathing cycles. The caravan park owner met them at the shore with his utility vehicle where they loaded John in the same manner, negotiating waves and heavy rain. The tray was too short and John's legs dangled off the back. CPR continued on the tray of the vehicle for a drive of approximately 1km. Once they arrived at the tourist camp, where the medical helicopter was to land, John showed weak vital signs. Kevin could not feel a pulse as his hands were numb from the rain and compressions. Others were asked to check as well, but none could confirm. They found a tarp to cover him from the rain so they could dry the skin and attempt use of the defibrillator. The defib was attached, and its automatic check advised that no shock was to be given. They were still on the tray of the vehicle, with rain pouring in from the edge of the tarp. John now had irregular, shallow and gasping breaths. Kevin placed him in the recovery position. They relocated the vehicle to find a bit more shelter with a bigger tarp, choosing not to move him again in his fragile condition, but to keep him dry and monitor him closely.

An ambulance arrived. The helicopter was delayed, likely due to the poor weather. The ambulance attendants took over care for John, and Kevin relayed all details. The helicopter landed next, but they decided to transport John by vehicle instead.

They were off in a blaze of sirens, dampened by the wind and heavy rain.

John survived his ordeal. He woke in hospital with burns to his hands and feet. The first thing he asked for was scrambled eggs. Once John was secure, and the adrenaline slowly seeped from his body, Kevin sat alone, head in hands. Thinking of his wife and baby son, he kept repeating to himself, "It could have been me."

A moment can snatch a life. A moment can save a life.

Are we ever ready for an unexpected final moment? When we soar close to the edge of death – so close we can feel it graze our cheek – are we satisfied we have lived our life well enough to have earned an ending without regrets?

These were Kevin's thoughts as he relived the moment, wondering if he'd done enough. And then the slick slide into fantasy "what if it had been me? What then? What if?"

Kevin and John's story is remarkable.

One man survived a lightning strike with the odds stacked against him: on a remote island, with bad mobile reception in a vicious storm, with the miraculous coincidence of a resupply ship appearing in the nick of time. Another man, after nearly being zapped himself, had presence of mind to perform life-saving CPR in less than ideal circumstances for 40 minutes.

While lightning strikes can produce severe injuries, 90 per cent of people struck by lightning survive – if they receive prompt and immediate medical intervention. In Australia, it is estimated there are five to ten deaths, and over 100 severe injuries caused by lightning every year. [41] If we take preventive measures (stay out of water, away from trees, take shelter), and we do happen to be hit, it is likely we will survive.

This story encourages important self-reflection questions:

If it had been me, and I had been struck by lightning and not survived, would I be content that I had lived my life well? Am I living each moment fully? When the Grim Reaper comes for me, will I be empty of regret? Have I developed enough heart so that I can reach out to another? Do I have the courage to act?

This story reminds us to live more fully, in deep self-awareness, and to make the most of each moment.

Insight

Connection and kindness on a city street corner

I knew he wasn't long for this world. He was skinny and gaunt, with leathery and lifeless skin, crinkled from years of narrow focus on survival. His eyes were crystal blue – the kind that make you believe in angels. Though his were haunted by ghosts. You could tell the angels were trying to look after him, but he did not feel them.

Scrubby worked the corner of Northbourne and Antill Street as a street window screen washer or 'scrubber.' He was there, day in day out.

I always gritted my teeth, trying to give the 'go away – not me' vibe. It never worked. He always hobbled over, raising his squeegee with a polite inquiring look. Then I felt obliged to cough up some change.

It really annoyed me – the sense of obligation for service I didn't really want, and did not know how to say no to without feeling like an asshole. After all, the guy was clearly a drug addict with his pin-pricked eyes. I knew I was supporting drugs and self-destruction every time I handed him my 50 cents.

As Scrubby's corner was the unavoidable stop on my way home

from the gym, every morning I warred with myself over what was the right thing to do. If I sped up just enough I'd sail through the lights and avoid him. Or if I waited at the corner long enough I'd be too far along in the queue to have to deal with it. Problem solved.

Eventually, I made an uneasy agreement with myself about the situation. If Scrubby came up to my window, I would talk to him as another human being, and honour the socially-pressured-I-know-it-might-be-wrong-but-I-don't-know-what-else-to-do-without-feeling-like-a-bitch-decision of handing over some coins.

Over time, I learned his name was Ian. That's about all I knew of him. When he showed up after a brief absence with a pronounced limp, I thought, "I bet his dealer beat the crap out of him for not paying a debt or something."

I asked him about it and he said, "It's an old footy injury, Miss." Apart from the bizarre thrill of being called 'Miss' despite my obvious matronly years of well past my forties, I was stopped by his comments. I knew, and he knew it was not an old footy injury. He had been harmed in some way by bad people, for bad things.

And yet there was something in Scrubby that clung to another identity, a sense of decorum and an old life left behind. He probably did play football at one time, before things went badly. Part of him had a string of memory for a life where he played football, where the world treated him with respect. He was always so polite. He did not push the squeegee on people with any rancour or threat; sometimes he just washed the window because he could. Sometimes he did this for me even though I warned him I had run out of coins (truthfully).

I came to enjoy the little snapshots of his world. I admired his determination and focus to show up every day, even when it was raining. Who gets their windscreen washed when it rains? He spoke of his day, of it being hot, of it being quiet, of it being chilly. Someone from a construction company had given him a high-visibility vest to wear so he wouldn't get smacked by a car as he hobbled between them at the light changes.

I'm sure some people were rude and brushed him away with

a dismissive hand. He did not seem to spend too much time worrying about them, just moved away to the next vehicle.

Whenever I gave him some coins, he always said, "It's kind to tip, Miss."

Those words sifted through my consciousness. Was it a kindness to tip? I'm still not sure whether or not I was helping perpetuate the cycle of poverty, despair and drugs, or whether it was indeed a kindness. I'd like to say I did out of the kindness of my heart, but truthfully, most of the time, it was out of guilt and a sense of social obligation. It's a cultural expectation. Knowing this consciously did not alleviate the angst, but only made it worse.

I returned from a trip away and noticed flowers tied to the traffic light pole at his usual corner. That kind of tribute only meant one thing: Scrubby was gone.

I burst into tears. It might have been the fatigue of the trip, I don't know. I only know that at the moment I felt a sense of loss for his passing. A life gone like the wisp of smoke. It wasn't a shock. Looking at his thin limbs with paper-thin skin from dehydration and poor nutrition, I could tell his body would surrender at some point.

There was an article in the *Canberra Times* about his passing. Scrubby was a well-known character in the community. It turns out he was from a well-off family, went to a private school, and did indeed play football. He'd lost both his parents when he was a teenager. Subsequently, this led to his less-than-sensible choices. I cried more reading this. I imagine a young Scrubby, or Ian, as a young man suddenly cast adrift in the world without guidance. The sense of loss and abandonment would have been enormous. Fear, loneliness, and grief possibly led him to drugs.

And yet years later, traces of his past life bubbled to the surface. A polite street corner window washer with an old footy injury.

I was glad that I had made some effort to see him as human, to really see him as an individual, in spite of my inner wrangling of righteousness. We don't get these moments back. When we look at another human being, we always have the choice to connect, to really see them. These are small moments where a kindness can help ease a life of pain. It costs us nothing but letting go of our judgements.

It costs us nothing but to show up and be real.

35. Creating connected leadership

Leadership training is not going to save us. We don't need more leadership models and theories. We need a transformation of leadership thinking, being, and doing.

What we need is leaders who can be here, right now. We need leaders who can see the present moment in all its vibrant detail. We need leaders who can also hold the vast complexity of history that has tilted the universe to this very point in time. We need leaders who can be in the space of tension and terror, yet speak and move calmly through it, carrying us all.

We need leaders who can connect – with others, with themselves, with the whole of humanity and the world.

We need leaders who can make a decision in the moment, who can connect in the moment, who can take action in the moment.

We need leaders who choose to treat every moment as a defining moment.

It's the small gestures that make a moment a defining moment. It's the smile we give to the busker on the corner. It's when we stop in the hallway and praise someone for a job well done. It's the phone call to say thank you. It's the touch on the shoulder for someone who is caught in grief. It's the hug we give our child when they are distressed over a lost teddy.

Every moment is a defining moment. How we show up, what we do, what we say, the energy we radiate: these all define who we are and how we influence our world, and thus the world.

Leadership is not the big presentation or the speech from the lectern. It's not even the finish line of the race. It's all the tiny moments strung together like beads on a necklace that make the moment beautiful. And powerful.

An Olympic athlete trains for hundreds of hours, week after week, year after year, for their short moment in the sun. It's all the choices they made, in each of those moments, that make the ultimate moment. It's choosing to push harder when they could have backed off. It's showing up for training when they'd rather be swinging in a hammock. It's deciding every day to be an Olympic athlete and living their thoughts and choices through that identity.

If we choose today to be a conscious leader who shows up each moment with the intention to serve humanity from a world-centric perspective, then we will have shifted the planet for peace and prosperity. Every day we choose to do our best, be our best, think our best. And as a result, every day our best gets better.

Leadership happens in moments, not meetings. Connected leadership is grounded and electric. Connected leadership allows us to harness a lightning strike during turbulent times of change. Change can be an electric pulse that blows everything clear. It commands attention. It illuminates. It stops us in our tracks and brings our focus to the immediate. Connected leaders know how to prepare for such moments, and how to be the lightning rod that redirects the energy safely.

Connected leaders don't need a crisis to command attention. Connected leaders have cut through, like the chime of a Tibetan bell. We have strong presence, we have an expanded and focused perspective, and we have the power do what is needed when it matters most.

Real moments

Being seen, heard, and valued begins with you. It's about how you see yourself, how you manage your personal choices and your inner voice. It's about how you carry yourself in any interaction and the intention you bring with you to those interactions. When you see and hear yourself truly, you will value yourself. When you reach this state of self-awareness and appreciation, others will know it too. You won't impress anyone, you will connect with them. This is the art and currency of influence.

Self-conscious leadership is still self-oriented. If we move past self-consciousness, from being nice or raw to being real, we move in to a whole new way of leading with others.

Being real in leadership means we own all of ourselves. We don't need to be vulnerable, as we've evolved past that stage. We know who we are, we have confronted our dark side, made peace with it, and can now activate the best part of ourselves while not denying the dark side. By being real, we are completely centered, fully open, and fully engaged with others. By being real, we allow others to show up as they are, give them permission to be all of who they are without any judgement. We create safety in relationships because we feel safe with ourselves.

By being real, we create a new power. It's the power of calling ourselves and others to be fully self-expressed and fully present as a result. This kind of power is deep influence – one that is not power over (command and control), or power on (being nice or pretending to be), or power in (vulnerability), but power *with*. When we are real we connect deeply, we co-create with others, and together we build possibilities. We are liberated. In being real, we are free.

– ¤ –

When you feel the dawn reach in and gently bring you from your dreams, savour the moment. You have another day alive on this glorious planet. Another day to breathe air, to feel the caress of wind, to witness the miracle of nature, to delight in the dance of humanity.

Imagine each day as a discovery of life and living. Each moment is an opportunity to explore the vastness of human life. Each moment is an opportunity to focus through joy and peace. Each moment is an opportunity to practice compassion. Each moment is an opportunity to be a kinder, better version of yourself.

Each moment is a moment that matters. Be gentle on yourself and allow yourself to enjoy it.

Next Steps

Staying inspired and focused is a discipline. It's easier when you have company! Here are some inspirational and practical ways to build your conscious leadership capacities with Zoë Routh.

The Blog: Inspiring articles to share and encourage leaders to be their best in the moments that matter.

The Podcast: The Zoë Routh Leadership Podcast will keep you evolving while you drive or slog it out on the treadmill.

The Tube: The Zoë Routh Leadership Moments YouTube channel to nudge your leadership evolution.

www.facebook.com/zoe.routh

www.linkedin.com/in/zoerouth

@zoerouth

@zoerouth

Executive Coaching

Zoë shows leaders how to lead with grace. Together, we focus on depth of thinking, effectiveness of action, and quality of presence. Various programs are tailored to you, depending on your stage of leadership development and sphere of influence.

Get outdoors with the Leadership Circle

Zoë's Group Mastermind training with executive coaching starts with a three-day expedition in a beautiful location such as the Larapinta Trail near Alice Springs Australia. Senior leaders come together in inspiring locations to create the time and space for quality reflection, and planning for business and self-development. Under the stars and sun, the Group Mastermind is about connection, reflection, and traction.

Team Development

Workshops and development programs for new teams, re-formed teams, or ambitious powerhouse teams. Zoë combines the wisdom of the wilderness with the cauldron of the classroom to help teams get real with each other. Leaders will experience collaborative conversations and relationships to advance the work that inspires you.

Zoë Routh
zoerouth.com

Acknowledgments

Writing the second book was just as arduous the first one, and needed the team to help me bring this baby to fruition.

To my A-Team: Bianca Jurd and Lisa Wilmott. Thanks for keeping the ship floating! Bringing this work to the world is so much easier and way more fun in your company.

Thanks to my ace editor, Rebecca Stewart, for planting seeds of awesomenesss in my brain, and for helping tame this literary beast in to something far more sensible and easier to read.

For Rob, for being brave alongside me and allowing me to share our personal stories. And for keeping me laughing and real when I get too serious.

For all my fellow travellers in the Thought Leaders Business School community, when you share your courage and aspirations, when you pick yourself up after a disappointment, when you remain committed to the difference you were born to make and show up to be seen, heard, and valued because you see, hear and value others – well, you take my breath away. I am elevated by the company I keep.

To Matt Church and Peter Cook, thanks for your leadership and support, and for being glorious men and models of abundance and generosity.

For my wonderful mentor, Dermot Crowley, whose humility and kindness is knit into every cell of your being, thank you for being so damn insightful.

For my family, for being the home that needs no geographical boundary. You are with me every day in every way that counts.

For my clients and for all who dare to be truth-tellers: your courage, conviction, and connection is making this world a better place for us all. With all my heart – thank you for being a leading light.

About the Author

Zoë Routh is a leadership mentor and speaker who shows people how to work better together.

She is English-born, Canadian-raised, and Australian-adopted; an Outdoor Adventurist and Experiential Educator, Truth Teller, Learner, Cancer Dancer, One-Time Belly Dancer, Aspiring Telemark Skier, Slayer of Dragons, and Mother of Chickens.

Zoë began her career leading canoe trips through the rugged Canadian wilderness. In 1996 she moved to Australia to work with Outward Bound, where she developed nationally-recognised outdoor leadership training programs. Furthering her passion for people and learning, with the Australian Rural Leadership Foundation she developed industry leadership programs for the wine, rice, and mining communities.

Zoë works closely with senior leaders in higher education, the private sector, rural industry groups, and the public service. Her high-impact leadership learning programs take place indoors and outdoors in spectacular settings.

As a high energy and engaging speaker, Zoë presents frequently to industry groups and organisations on the future of leadership.

Read more about Zoë's work at **www.zoerouth.com**

Endnotes

1. Campbell, J., 2008. *The Hero with a Thousand Faces* (The Collected Works of Joseph Campbell). 3rd edition. Novato: New World Library.

2. Aaron Ralston was a solo adventurer. On one fateful adventure he had his hand caught between a fallen boulder and a canyon wall. Realising no help would come before he died of exposure and dehydration, he took the drastic step of breaking his wrist bones, and sawing through the skin and remaining ligaments and bone fragments to free himself. He survived and continues to adventure solo.

3. All the case studies and stories in *Moments* are genuine accounts. In most accounts I have changed names and sometimes the gender of the person to protect their privacy.

4. gamertherapist.com/blog/2013/08/25/dopey-about-dopamine-video-games-drugs-addiction-2/

5. en.wikipedia.org/wiki/Enron_scandal

6. en.wikipedia.org/wiki/Jeffrey_Skilling

7. www.afr.com/business/transport/automobile/volkswagen-ceo-winterkorn-resigns-amid-emissions-cheating-scandal-20150923-gjtlij

8. www.bbc.com/news/business-34324772

9. hdr.undp.org/sites/default/files/ranking.pdf

10. Garner, Janine, 2015. *From Me To We – Why commercial collaboration will future proof business, leaders, and personal success.* Melbourne: Wiley.

11. www.space.com/31388-elon-musk-colonize-mars-now.html

12. www.gwava.com/blog/internet-data-created-daily

13. http-download.intuit.com/http.intuit/CMO/intuit/
    futureofsmallbusiness/intuit_2020_report.pdf

14. Diamandis, Peter M., Kotler, Steven, 2012. *Abundance –
    The Future Is Better Than You Think.* New York: Free Press.

15. Carnegie, Dale, 1936, 1964, 1981, 2006. *How to Win Friends and
    Influence People.* London: Vermillion.

16. Brown, Brené, 2005. *Rising Strong.* London: Vermilion.

17. hbr.org/2002/09/crucibles-of-leadership

18. Covey, Stephen, 1989, 2004, 2013. *The 7 Habits of Highly Effective
    People.* Rosetta Books.

19. Campbell, J., 2008. *The Hero with a Thousand Faces*
    (The Collected Works of Joseph Campbell). 3rd edition. Novato:
    New World Library.

20. Pitt, Turia with Harkness, Libby, 2013. *Everything To Live For.*
    Sydney: Random House.

21. Ditto

22. Read more about Eckhart Tolle here: www.eckharttolle.com

23. The Harry Potter series is one of the most successful literary
    series ever written, then made into a series of movies, eight at last
    count.

24. Hat tip to the brilliant Dr Jason Fox for extolling on the key
    premise of making progress visible as a key motivating factor in
    his book, *The Game Changer.* 2014. Melbourne: Wiley.

25. www.johnmaxwell.com/blog/teamwork-and-vision-go-hand-
    in-hand

26. Yousafzai, Malala with Lamb, Christina, 2013. *I am Malala – The
    girl who stood up for education and was shot by the Taliban.*
    London: Weidenfield & Nicholson.

27. Cialdini, Robert, 1984, 1994, 2007, 2009. *Influence: The Psychology
    of Persuasion.* Sydney: Harper Collins.

28. Brown, Brené, 2005. *Rising Strong.* London: Vermilion.

29. Torbert, Bill, 2004. *Action Inquiry – The Secret of Timely and Transforming Leadership.* San Francisco: Berrett-Koehler Publishers, Inc.

30. Wilber, Ken, Patten, Terry, Leonard, Adam, Morelli, Marco, 2012. *Integral Life Practice – A 21st Century Blueprint for Physical Health, Emotional Balance, Mental Clarity, and Spiritual Awakening.* Boston: Integral Books.

31. www.theaustralian.com.au/opinion/columnists/paul-kelly/ the-tragedy-of-kevin-rudd-can-be-traced-to-a-personality-flaw/ news-story/1ce99fd6672a5b6359f269e34a032666

32. Cuddy, Amy, 2015. *Presence – Bringing Your Boldest Self To Your Biggest Challenges.* London: Orion Books.

33. Whitsett, David, Dolgener, Forrest, Mabon Kole, Tanjala, 1998. *The Non-Runner's Marathon Trainer.* Chicago: Masters Press.

34. www.theintentionexperiment.com

35. www.masaru-emoto.net

36. Fox, Dr Jason, 2016. *How to Lead A Quest – A handbook for pioneering executives.* Melbourne: Wiley.

37. Hill, Darren, Hill, Alison, Richardson, Dr Sean, 2016. *Dealing With The Tough Stuff – How to achieve results from key conversations.* Melbourne: Wiley.

38. Rodenberg, Patsy, 2007. *Presence: How to use positive energy for success in every situation,* London: Penguin.

39. Sandberg, Sheryl, 2013. *Lean In – Women, Work, and the Will To Lead.* London: Random House.

40. Wilber, Ken, Patten, Terry, Leonard, Adam, Morelli, Marco, 2012. *Integral Life Practice – A 21st Century Blueprint for Physical Health, Emotional Balance, Mental Clarity, and Spiritual Awakening.* Boston: Integral Books.

41. www.australiawidefirstaid.com.au/lightning-strikes/

COMPOSURE

HOW CENTERED LEADERS MAKE THE BIGGEST IMPACT

More than ever, leaders need grace under fire. This is the ability to stay calm when all else is in chaos. This is the leader's handbook for developing wise and compassionate leadership, regardless of circumstances.

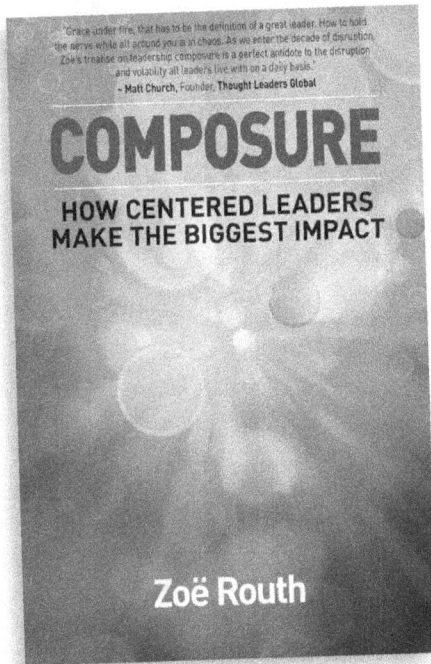

Get your copy at

Zoë Routh

zoerouth.com

Notes

Notes

www.ingramcontent.com/pod-product-compliance
Lightning Source LLC
Chambersburg PA
CBHW070725220326
41598CB00024BA/3305